PARTY
CONFIDENTIAL

Lara Shriftman and Elizabeth Harrison

WITH LARA MORGENSON

PHOTOS BY JEFF VESPA AND WIREIMAGE

BULFINCH PRESS

NEW YORK • BOSTON

INTRODUCTION

THE PARTIES

FROM OUR FILES

RECIPES

introduction

t's your best friend's birthday and you want to throw something fabulous, chic, and out of the ordinary. Another wine and cheese party? Blah. Backyard barbecue? Nothing new there. All of a sudden it becomes too much money, too much planning, and *way* too much stress. Just the thought of throwing a party is enough to send people into a complete panic. They moan about cost, what to serve, how to decorate, and, omigod, what to do. We're here to put these fears to rest and show you that throwing fantastic parties is fun, easy, and doable on any budget. As experts with thousands of events to our names, we're here to demystify the party-planning process. We designed *Party Confidential* to show you how we plan parties, from beginning to end. Packed with imaginative tips and ideas, this book is written for anyone from the age of eight to eighty, with budgets ranging from fifty to five hundred thousand dollars. You don't have to be Sean "Diddy" Combs to throw a smashing soiree!

Our first books, *Fête Accompli! The Ultimate Guide to Creative Entertaining* and the accompanying workbook *The Ultimate Party Planning Guide*, were created as textbooks to teach you the art of entertaining. In this book we offer visual inspiration that will help you plan new and unique parties and encourage you to think outside the box. Instead of throwing a traditional birthday celebration, make the occasion a sugar party or a fabulous disco bash! We selected ten of our favorite concepts to get you inspired, including a nightclub party introducing Paris Hilton's perfume, a shopping party at a boutique, an authentic Indian feast, an organic dinner, and a casual afternoon dog party.

Each of the ten chapters features a different concept and outlines each element in detail: the invite, location, menu, sound, décor, lighting, flowers, and gift bags. You can splurge and do it like we did or steal the idea and make it your own for a lot less money. Can't afford thirty kickboard invitations for your pool party? No problem; make a splash with beach balls or bottles of suntan oil. Ultimately, it's about making a unique statement; we just provide you with the suggestions and tools to go out and make it happen. You can take as much or as little from each concept and apply your own twist. Realize that for every one idea there are a million options!

In addition to our step-by-step party guide, we dedicate an entire section to food-and-drink recipes from the caterers that did our events, celebrities, and yummy restaurants such as Mr. Chow, the Forge, Pop Burger, and the infamous nightclub Privé. Some recipes were served at our parties, others are suggestions just for you. For when you get down to the nitty-gritty of spending your hard-earned bucks on decorations and more, we've put together a comprehensive resource guide to help you purchase everything from customized invitations to vintage serving platters. The book features our top ten no-fail party tips as well as info on how to give a great toast, plan a budget, and turn any party into a fund-raiser. We even asked our better-known friends for their advice. You'll find fabulous words of party wisdom from pros like David Arquette, Lara Flynn Boyle, Billy Bob Thornton, Molly Sims, and Luke Wilson.

So what are you waiting for? **Let's get this party started!**

Elizabeth Harrison
and Lara Shriftman

10 no-fail party tips

Overinvite! Let's face it, people—even your best friend in the whole world—can flake. Maybe they've had a terrible week at work, a family crisis, or an unexpected guest; whatever the reason, no-shows and last-minute cancellations are bound to happen. Plus, people will come late and others will leave early, so when putting together your guest list use this rule of thumb: Invite 5 extra people for every 20.

On the List The key to a great party is having an interesting mix of people. Think about it: Everyone wants to see old friends *and* meet new people. Expand your social circle by browsing your e-mail list and phone book, and ask your best friends and coworkers to invite friends and acquaintances.

Money Matters Once you've decided to have a party and selected a theme and the number of guests, it's time to set a budget! Decide what is most important to you—is it crystal serving glasses? blossoms to die for? or insane invites? Be prepared for overage by reserving 10–15 percent of your budget for anything you might forget and/or those last-minute ideas that drive up the cost.

Where It's At Pick a fabulous location that people will love, such as an old classic, a hot new trendy bar, or an amazing home that has people itching for a peek. For example, we threw our Juicy Couture pool party on the grounds of the Burndorf Estate, where scenes from *Mommie Dearest* were filmed, while for our Indian theme party, the chance to see Brian and Gigi Grazer's gorgeous estate was enough to guarantee RSVPs.

Timing Is Everything We always like to give both a start and an end time to our parties; if you keep the night open-ended, people will trickle in all night long, whereas if the invite specifies 7–9:00 p.m., guests are more likely to arrive earlier and stay longer because everyone will be there around the same time. Avoid having a long time frame or you will offset the flow of guests. For example, with a four-hour party, you'll have a fantastically crowded three-plus hours, but if the party stretches from 8:00 p.m.–2:00 a.m., people will come and go all night long, leaving you with loads of downtime.

Thirst Quenchers Be sure to have plenty of nonalcoholic beverages for the designated drivers, mamas-to-be, and others who aren't in the imbibing frame of mind. At the end of the evening, we like to serve flavored coffees, cappuccino, and espresso as our guests head out the door or wait at the valet. And don't forget to have ample amounts of bottled water on hand.

Greet Guests with a Cocktail At Harrison & Shriftman events, we always station a number of servers at the entrance with a tray of drinks both alcoholic and nonalcoholic. Better yet, create a signature cocktail for the evening like we did for our classic cocktail party.

Go Mini! Forget the buffet tables—there's nothing worse than balancing a plate of food, silverware, *and* a drink. Maximize comfort by passing bite-sized hors d'oeuvres like mini-hamburgers, sushi, and tiny sandwiches.

Salty 'n' Sweet A party is not the place to be diet conscious, so give your guests the chance to splurge. Offer a decadent balance of savory treats like coconut shrimp and French fries and sugar delicacies like cupcakes and candy. Now that's finger-lickin' good!

Dress Rehearsal Okay, you don't have to actually put on your party dress, but a week before the party, do a run-through so you have plenty of time to solve any unexpected problems. Do another run-through the day before and the day of the party to be absolutely certain you didn't forget a single thing. Practice will make it perfect.

Peter Som's fall
fashion party at
Elana Posner's
house for
Quest magazine.

Organically
Good
A Dinner Party at Home

(From left) Forest and Keisha Whitaker, Lara Shriftman, Dr. Alejandro Junger, chef Akasha Richmond, Catherine Gordon, Tierney Gearon, and Lara Morgenson toast to a wonderful meal.

Akasha Richmond caters events and parties in Los Angeles and is also the celebrity chef for White Wave's Silk soy milk. She has served her recipes at the Environmental Media Association awards, backstage at the Grammys and Farm Aid, and at ChefDance during the Sundance Film Festival. Some of her favorite experiences include: preparing meals for **Barbra Streisand,** cooking holiday dinners for **Billy Bob Thornton,** making Thanksgiving dinner for two hundred while on tour with **Michael Jackson,** and catering parties for **Pierce Brosnan.** Her cookbook is titled *Hollywood Dish.*

Dinner parties are such a great way to entertain, whether they are casual or formal, at home or in a restaurant. But the stakes are certainly higher when cooking up a three-course, five-star meal at your cushy pad. It doesn't matter if you're the resident Martha Stewart in your group or a party-planning novice; everyone gets nervous. Setting the table, worrying about how the meal will come out—all of these things can cause heart palpitations. But just take a deep breath and get organized. You *can* do a dinner party for ten, fifty, or even two hundred as long as you know *what* you want and are well prepared for the event.

We threw an Organic Dinner Party at a private home in the Hollywood Hills for ten of our earth-lovin' friends. The fabulously talented chef Akasha Richmond, who specializes in organic cooking, created a classic menu with ingredients fresh from the farmers' market. Guests began arriving for cocktails at 8:00 p.m., and after a short time nibbling on cheese and crackers, we settled into the dining room for a delicious three-course meal. Keep in mind that your cocktails should be served, at most, for only one hour.

This chapter is a great springboard since every concept can be adapted for gatherings of any size, whether you want to invite eight of your closest friends or hold a massive reception with a hundred of your nearest and dearest. What're ya waiting for? Get cooking!

The key to getting a Michelin rating?

Don't try to do everything yourself. Help is one of the major ingredients to a successful dinner party. Ask friends to pitch in or a housekeeper to be present, or hire a caterer so you can entertain your guests. Remember, as the host it's your job to make introductions and keep the conversation flowing and the food and drink a-comin'. Recruit a cohost; that way you can run to the kitchen without deserting your guests.

CHIC TIP
ALWAYS DO A TRIAL RUN THE DAY BEFORE THE PARTY TO MAKE SURE YOU HAVE ENOUGH PLACE SETTINGS, GLASSES, AND SERVING DISHES. AND IT'S ALWAYS GOOD TO HAVE AT LEAST FIVE EXTRA PLACE SETTINGS— AND TONS OF EXTRA GLASSES—ON HAND. AN UNEXPECTED GUEST COULD SHOW UP, A PLACE SETTING COULD BREAK, AND SO ON.

One of the most important parts of a dinner party is how the food is styled. Make it look elegant by carefully positioning each ingredient and wiping off any dribbles or smears. And, of course, think about unique serving pieces and layering the colors.

Location

A dinner party doesn't have to be at home. If you don't have a space large enough or that suits your needs, find a restaurant that does. But when doing so, there are some questions to settle. Like, how will you decide on a meal that pleases every single person's palate? You've got to think about the vegan at the table, the anticarb girls, and the ravenous meat eaters.

The best solution is to select, always ahead of time (you don't want guests just ordering off the menu or you will spend a fortune), three to four entrées that the guests can choose from. Include a vegetarian, a fish, and a meat option. Or forgo that headache and serve it all family-style. Whichever method you decide on, just be sure to negotiate the fee ahead of time with the restaurant manager or owner. And don't forget to include beverages in the cost. Do you want wine only or a full bar? All of these points need to be considered (check out p. 149 for more info on contracts).

How to Properly Set the Table

There's no bigger faux pas than a table that is set incorrectly. So avoid any fork mishaps by following our rules. Remember, the silverware is used from the outside in: appetizer fork leads to salad fork leads to entrée fork and so on.

1. Start with dinner plates and layer as follows: The entrée dish goes under the salad plate.

2. Place the salad and dinner forks to the left of the dinner plate, with the dinner fork closer to the plate.

3. On the right side sits the knife, next to the spoon and on the inside.

4. The bread-and-butter plate should be substantially smaller than the dinner plate and should rest, with its own butter knife, to the left of the dinner plate.

5. Position the dessert fork and spoon at twelve o'clock, or at the top of the dinner plate, resting horizontally.

6. Place glasses in the upper right corner. They progress by size from left to right: water glass, red-wine glass, white-wine glass, dessert-wine glass.

7. After the dinner plates have been cleared, you can then place dessert plates and coffee cups and saucers on the table in front of each person.

Create a Seating Chart

1. Create a sketch of your tables.

2. Figure out how many people each table can comfortably accommodate.

3. Enlarge the seating chart on a photocopier and number each table. Laminate the chart at a local copy store.

4. Write down each guest's name on small round labels in two colors (one for the guys and the other for the girls). Group the names into sets of six, eight, ten, or however many will be seated at each table.

5. Begin assigning tables by placing the groups onto your chart. Since the chart is laminated, it's easy to move the labels around. If you're planning a ritzy soiree, pay attention to where each table is located before assigning an A-lister to a table in the back.

6. Once you've settled on the perfect seating arrangement, begin numbering or naming the tables.

7. Do an "idiot check." Go through each name on your master guest list and make sure each one has an assigned place.

8. Plan ahead for unexpected guests by stockpiling a bunch of extra chairs. This way, if the bachelor-for-life shows up with a date, you'll have a seat for her!

CHIC TIP

AFTER DINNER YOU CAN EITHER END THE PARTY OR TURN IT UP, DEPENDING ON YOUR PLANS FOR THE EVENING. YOU CAN GO UPBEAT WITH CLUB MUSIC AND GET GUESTS READY FOR A LATE NIGHT, OR YOU CAN WIND THE PARTY DOWN WITH MELLOW SOUNDS. GUESTS STILL HANGING AROUND? TURN THE LIGHTS UP. IT'S THE UNIVERSAL SIGNAL FOR "THIS NIGHT IS OV-AH."

The most important part of any dinner party is how you set the table. Combine the expected with the unexpected. We used mirrors as serving platters and lit votive candles.

How to Create Six Tiers of Blossoms

You will need:

Green floral foam (available from floral supply stores)

Six-tiered cake tray or any multilevel serving piece

Enough roses (or any other blossom) to fill the six tiers.

Tier Up

1. Soak the green foam in a bucket of water until it is thoroughly saturated.

2. Take a sharp knife and cut the foam to fit each level of the tray.

3. Cut the stems down to about two inches.

4. Working in a circle around the tray, poke the stems into the green foam. Repeat with each layer. The flowers will be two to three layers deep on each tier. Make sure every inch is covered in blossoms.

Note: This lovely centerpiece can be obstructive. Display it on the table until the dinner begins, then move it to the living room or wherever you adjourn for coffee and after-dinner drinks.

CHIC TIP
MAKE USE OF EVERY SINGLE BLOSSOM! WE TOOK EXTRA FLOWERS AND ARRANGED THEM IN SILVER GIMLET GLASSES AROUND THE DISPLAY.

The Playlist

Low ambient music is the base for any dinner party. You want it to be upbeat but at the same time completely unobtrusive to conversation. Save the party beats for the late-night afterparty! We played Latin music from Edgard Varèse and a bit of soft jazz. Keep in mind the kind of vibe you want for your dinner party and pick music that matches that mood. Below are some of our best picks for dinner-party tunes.

Latin music from **Viejas Locas** and **Marc Lavoine**

The Opera Album featuring Maria Callas, Roberto Alagna, Luciano Pavarotti, Placido Domingo, and more

Anything jazz. We like the compilation *Jazz Vocal Essentials*, volume 2

Modern soft rock from Liz Phair, Coldplay, Norah Jones, Jack Johnson, Enya, and others

Music soundtracks including *Cinema Paradiso*, *Frida*, and *Garden State*

Billy Bob Thornton's Music Tip for Dinner Parties: THE BEATLES' *REVOLVER* AND *RUBBER SOUL*

Lighting

The right lighting will make your guests, the food, and the room look incredible, so think about it carefully. Make the ambience sexy and chic with softly dimmed lights and flickering candles. Don't go overboard and make it too dark—people want to see what they are eating, and they want to see the guest across the table! Just make it soft and subtle.

Steal It!

Dim the lights. If your switches don't have dimmers, replace lightbulbs with lower-wattage bulbs in soft amber and rose hues.

Play with your color theme. We added splashes of red to black and white, so the white votive candles on the dinner table were in red holders.

Use unscented candles so that the only aroma is from the delicious dinner. If you do want a scent, pick one and one only and keep it soft and subtle, like gardenia or vanilla. Better yet, wait until after the main course to light a scented candle or set out the aroma sticks.

Don't forget the other rooms! Light a scented candle in the bathroom and the hallway leading to the dining room.

If you have a lovely view, pull back the curtains and rest votive candles on the windowsills.

The table is the center of attention at a dinner party, so make it as gorgeous as possible. We set the table in black, white, and splashes of red. This beautiful display of roses was designed by our favorite florist, Eric Buterbaugh. You can take nearly anything, from a birdbath to champagne glasses, and turn it into a centerpiece.

How to Overinvite

As you write up your guest list, keep in mind that you can't count on every person you invite to attend. Yes, people get busy at the last minute, and there are inevitably excuses (most of them good!). At one party, we had someone cancel at the last minute and another couple arrived over an hour late, so by adding a few extras you're assured of a full table.

Guest Work

1. Send out invitations in two waves. Send the initial batch to your A-list crew; once you start finding out who can't make the date, put the B-list batch in the mail. This ensures a full—but not overly crowded—house.

2. Separate your guest list into two groups: the sure things and the maybes. Even people who have RSVP'd yes find that things come up at the last minute. Weigh the two groups against each other to see if you should send out additional invites. In the process, be sure to include plus-ones, which are guests of the guests.

3. For every twenty guests invited, add five more. If there's one thing we've learned in our years of party planning, it's that people cancel. Assume that out of twenty invites, three to five guests will be no-shows.

4. Do a time check. If your party is scheduled to last more than two hours, most likely you will have a turnover halfway through the evening. One group will arrive and leave earlier while a second set will show up later in the evening. If you want a full house throughout the night, take into consideration the habits of your guests and strive for an equal balance of early birds and night owls.

> "Always send thank-you notes, no matter what! In addition, always save a copy of your invite list. That way it's super easy for future parties to just hit 'add CC' on your computer."
> **—Molly Sims**

Invitations

We wanted something elegant and timeless, and nothing evokes this mood better than calligraphy invitations by Bernard Maisner. We sent out amazing black-and-white invites on a thick piece of high-quality card stock, in matching envelopes. Of course, with a dinner party you don't have to send out actual invitations—you could call people or even send an e-mail—but an old-school invitation makes the evening a bit more formal and adds a sophisticated touch.

Steal It!

If you decide to send out invitations, an elegant dinner party demands a timeless invite, so skip the gimmicks.

Use thick quality paper and a simple, clean design with neat lettering. Classic invites are typically four by six or five by seven inches in size.

Choose a traditional color palette: white, off-white, or cream card stock with navy, black, silver, or gold ink.

Select a font that is both curvy and artful, or a minimalist modern block. The layout of the text should be flush to the left or centered.

Use matching envelopes.

Name-Dropping

Don't forget to add place cards! If your event is formal, the card should match the invitation and use the same card stock, font, motifs, and colors to keep it consistent. For our dinner party, Bernard Maisner created elegant calligraphy designs for each setting, and at the end of the night the guests took their name card home. There are also many other things you can do to make the place card stand out as special.

Steal It!

Choose an object that blends with the theme of your party. For an Asian-inspired event, pick out a light-colored flat rock and write everyone's name on it in a bold color.

Select a beautiful, thick card stock and create fun shapes like stars or hearts. Tie them with a ribbon or string to water or wine glasses.

Attach a place card to the back of a chair with either a pin or a ribbon. Tuck a flower in for a bit of flair.

Print each person's name on a pretty ribbon and attach to a wineglass.

Frame a photograph of each guest and place at his or her seat.

Order Up

How to Select the Perfect Dinner at a Restaurant

Guests will show up with an empty stomach, so have a few appetizers for guests to nibble on upon their arrival. The key is to choose items that are tasty but not too filling, such as a vegetable platter with hummus. Keep in mind that the appetizers may be set out for a period of time, so pick things that won't get cold, runny, or undesirable after sitting out for an hour or longer.

No carbs? As if! Always offer warm, fresh baguettes or breadsticks with plenty of butter and dipping oils.

Choose a simple salad with a few ingredients, like a Caesar or baby mixed greens with a soft cheese. You can have the salad placed on the table before or after everyone has been seated. If you do it before, have the waiters bring out the salad dressing once everyone is seated so it stays chilled.

Decide how you want to serve the meal. You can do family style, which means all the dishes are placed in the center of the table so guests can help themselves, or have the waiters pass platters of each course and serve each guest. If you decide to have a preset menu where guests can choose their main course, the waiter will ask each guest his or her preference and serve the dinner on individual plates.

Order a variety of main courses. Serve at least one meat, fish, and vegetarian dish. Pasta is always a great vegetarian choice as it appeals to more than just the nonmeat eater.

Include at least three side dishes that are either placed or passed.

Opt for a dessert platter instead of individual plates. Not only will it cut down on the cost, but this way each guest will get a taste of the apple tartine, hazelnut gelato, and warm chocolate soufflé. In addition, place cake trays filled with cookies, mini-cupcakes, and petit fours on the table for guests to have with their coffee and after-dinner drinks.

Gift Bags

Simple, earthy gifts are best for an organic dinner party, and, of course, food is always an option. We filled a plain brown paper bag with:

Avalon Organics hand wash and lotion

Elixir Tonics & Teas loose-leaf teas, tonics, and recipe book

Napa Valley aged organic white-wine vinegar

365 Organic canola oil and **365 Organic** smooth almond butter

St. Claire's organic lime tarts

Stretch Island fruit leather

Green & Black's organic chocolate bars

Steal It!

Create a real goody bag filled with all-natural products. Include natural lotions, body washes, and candles as well.

Hand out a recipe for a dish or make a mini-cookbook with all the courses. Print the recipes on thick paper in a cool font or handwrite them on recipe cards. If you do more than one recipe, you can bind them in a photo album.

Akasha Richmond's book *Hollywood Dish* makes a wonderful gift.

Give a subscription to a magazine like *Vegetarian Times* or anything that fits the theme of your meal.

The Menu

Chef Akasha Richmond created an all-natural menu with wonderful winter ingredients. With the growth of local farmers' markets and specialty organic markets like Whole Foods, more and more people are choosing to eat healthier—it's all about hormone-free, free-range, and fresh-from-the-farm foods. The goal of an organic dinner is to celebrate local and seasonal ingredients. It's a great way to celebrate the local harvest or even to introduce others to eating the natural way.

While our dinner party had a seated, French butler–style service (food was plated in the kitchen and served by the course), there are a ton of serving options available. You can serve a bunch of small entrées with side dishes placed in the middle of the table so everyone can help himself or herself. And, of course, you can do a buffet-style dinner. The latter is more casual and informal, since guests can help themselves and picky eaters can choose what they like. But be careful: Don't leave the food sitting out unattended and have it out for only a certain period of time—not all night. Otherwise it sits there getting cold and unappealing.

CHIC TIP
ALWAYS CHECK WITH EVERY SINGLE PERSON ATTENDING YOUR DINNER PARTY AHEAD OF TIME AND FIND OUT IF ANYONE HAS ANY FOOD ALLERGIES—ESPECIALLY IF YOU'RE SERVING ANY OF THE USUAL SUSPECTS, LIKE NUTS OR SHELLFISH. NOTHING RUINS A DINNER PARTY LIKE A TRIP TO THE EMERGENCY ROOM!

ONE HOUR BEFORE DINNER

Assorted cheeses: brie, organic blue cheese rolled in chopped parsley, goat cheese rolled in crushed candied pecan nuts

365 Organic **cracked water crackers**

Nuts and olives served on a Crate and Barrel tray. We recommend organic Manzanillo olives by Mediterranean Organic, tree ripened, herbed, and whole

Vida Organica and Frey wines

FIRST COURSE

Carrot-ginger bisque with crispy shallots, served in demitasse cups on mirrors (recipe on page 159)

Earthbound Farm Organic mâche with persimmons, **candied walnuts** from Bristol Farms, **Papillon Roquefort**, and **pomegranate vinaigrette**

MAIN COURSE

Walnut-crusted salmon with fresh **pear salsa** (recipe on page 159)

Red quinoa with dried fruit

Brussels sprouts with **leeks** and **black mustard seeds**

Chunky **spiced-honey applesauce**

Herbed tofu or **tempeh**, as a vegetarian option

Desserts

Mont Blancs (meringues with chestnut puree and whipped cream)

Assorted **home-made cookies** and **soy milk**

Newman's Own cookies

Berries and **crème fraîche** served in martini or hurricane glasses

Drinks

Vida Organica rosé wine

Sauvignon blanc and natural red wines from Frey Organic Wines

Elixir Classic Tonics, including Depth Recharger, Liquid Yoga, Power Plant, Tame the Elements, and Virtual Buddha

Elixir loose-leaf teas

CHIC TIP
WE LOVE TO SERVE A PLATED DESSERT LIKE THE MONT BLANC AND THEN SET OUT BISCOTTI, PETIT FOURS, AND MINI-CUP-CAKES IN THE CENTER OF THE TABLE.

We served the carrot-ginger bisque with crispy shallots in demitasse cups on mirrors and played with the black-and-white color theme by serving the salad in a glass bowl set on a black plate. You can be whimsical, modern, or funky depending on what pieces you choose and how you combine them.

Oh, Sugar!
A Delicious Party

From snow cones to cookies and candy, a dream buffet for those with a sweet tooth.

A **Sugar Party is the perfect fix for a sweet tooth**—just ask Serena Williams! We were at her favorite sweet spot, Serendipity 3, in New York City, for their famous frozen hot chocolate when the inspiration hit us. What better way to give someone the perfect birthday surprise than to make it all about their favorite thing? So we dished up a sugar-spun party where Serena could indulge to her heart's content.

We invited fifty of her sweetest friends to join in on the sugar orgy and surprised Serena with a day straight out of her wildest dreams. She was thrilled when she arrived and saw the feast of desserts and fruity cocktails. We ordered tons and tons of old-school candies, so our spread included everything from carts serving snow cones and cotton candy to a buffet overflowing with goodies like treats from Dylan's Candy Bar, lollipops, and Pixy Stix. And we kept the pure sugar theme going by decorating Lara Shriftman's poolside backyard in all white.

The best thing about this type of party is that it doesn't have to be a stand-alone event. It can be the second half of your dinner party or the post-night-out-clubbing gathering. If you make it part of your dinner party, for example, after the meal is served ask your guests to retire to the living room, the outside patio, or the poolside and then unveil the sugar smorgasbord. Just be sure to warn your guests that all diets must be checked at the door!

Caution! Surprise parties are not for the weak of heart.

Be absolutely sure that the person won't be upset, and if you know they don't want to celebrate, *don't* plan a big to-do. Otherwise, be very specific when drawing up the guest list; you have to be able to anticipate whom they would want to be in attendance. Ask their best friend, boyfriend, mom, business assistant, or whomever they are close to for help—but go to more than one person so you have a well-rounded list. If you're a supersleuth try to get a peek at their e-mail address book or cell phone. Last, make sure the birthday girl or boy feels good, is dressed properly, and is in the mood to party.

Birthday girl
Serena Williams

Décor

White is the sugary color du jour, but you can play with any color you love. Pick the birthday boy's or girl's favorite, or pull a color from the candy they like best and go with it. We covered everything in white fabric and terry cloth, from the chaise longues and puffy pillows stacked poolside to a big plush bed piled high with pillows.

The candy takes center stage, so consider renting small tables and chairs to have more room to spread the candy out. We rented soda-shop chairs and tables, but picnic tables are a great addition to any backyard.

Steal It!

Buy large bolts of white terry cloth and go crazy covering your furniture.

Buy throw pillows or make slipcovers for ones that you already own.

Cover buffet tables and side tables in white tablecloths or spray paint inexpensive side tables.

Rent a cabana, create a tent from wispy curtains, or hang a hammock in the shade.

Move your bed outside and fill it with tons of pillows and add a few serving trays to hold drinks and treats.

WHAT'S YOUR BEST PARTY TIP?

"A good ratio of men to women."
— **Stephen Dorff**

"Have fun, be yourself, and don't worry about the stuffy people there!" — **Venus Williams**

"If it's a small gathering and is feeling stiff, never be scared to whip out the games."
— **Regina King**

Party Highlight: Smile! Our guests loved the photo booth we rented for the afternoon. They spent all day taking silly pictures and testing their best supermodel poses. A great option is to set up a Polaroid camera booth so you can easily snap pictures. Or just have tons of disposable cameras scattered around so guests can get snap happy.

WHO WAS THERE 1. Stephen Dorff and Quentin Tarantino **2.** Molly Sims **3.** Chris Heinz and Donovan Leitch **4.** Rachel Zalis, Beau Flynn, and Marley Shelton **5.** Serena Williams and Lorenz Tate **6.** Venus and Serena Williams **7.** Penny Marshall **8.** Kelly Rowland

Playlist

Eye of the Tiger: Don't forget the music! Serena's sister Lyndrea Price, a singer and songwriter, created this move-busting set of tunes to play during the relay games.

Can't Nobody by Kelly Rowland

December 4th by Jay Z

Work on Me by Lyndrea Price

Crazy in Love by Beyoncé

The Miseducation of Lauryn Hill by Lauryn Hill

Everything by Van Hunt

Get Rich or Die Tryin' by 50 Cent

Be by Common

Late Registration by Kanye West

Pumpin Thru Speakers by Lyndrea Price

Thriller by Michael Jackson

TP-2.com by R. Kelly

Urban Legend by T.I.

Speakerboxxx/The Love Below by Outkast

CrazySexyCool by TLC

Any album by Green Day

Goodies by Ciara

1

5

Invitations

The sugar high started early, with a big Dylan's Candy Bar lollipop attached to a boxed invitation. It was simple, *sweet,* and to the point. Since this was also a surprise party, we were sure to make that clear so that no one would ruin it. It's always best to follow up with each guest to make sure they are keeping their lips sealed and, most important, to remind them to be on time so they don't ruin the big moment.

Steal It!

Purchase boxed invitations that capture the sugar feeling or go for pure white card stock.

Print the details in a font like **PartyLET.**

Attach each invitation to a packet of sugar or a bag of candy, or wrap it around a chocolate bar—any sugary treat will do.

You can also print out party details on round Avery labels, run the labels through the printer, and then stick them on lollipops.

Serve It!

At our party the candy treats were passed around on trays and also set out for guests to nibble on at their leisure. Really think about how you present the treats. Create a gorgeous buffet, taking the candy out of the package and placing it in bowls of different sizes, colors, and heights. For example, stack bowls, use two- or three-tiered cake trays, decorate drink buckets with happy-birthday stickers, tie ribbons around glasses, and so on.

We filled big silver bowls with Red Hots, while clear acrylic trays with dividers held chocolate-dipped pretzels, toffee, and more. Pints of Ben & Jerry's ice cream were in restaurant-style serving dishes filled with ice, and ice-cream sandwiches rested in little silver bowls. Otter Pops were stuck in a tall glass with a ribbon tied around the base. And that's just for starters—you can use anything as a holder. Vases, votive-candle holders, and wineglasses are all options. Just make sure the mouth is wide enough for a hand to fit!

Steal It!

Use silver trays and platters, acrylic bowls, vases, candy boxes, and more. You don't have to buy everything; look around your home and use what you have.

Dress pieces up with a napkin or a ribbon, stickers, candy labels, or anything else you have on hand.

Sprinkle serving trays for drinks with little candies like Red Hots or SweeTarts.

Pass the treats on trays at first and then place them on tables throughout the venue. It's a good way to introduce menu items, and guests can splurge at their own pace.

Serve It!

A combination of drinks passed around on trays and self-serve drinks is best at casual parties. We had servers circulating with drinks and tons and tons of huge acrylic serving bowls filled with ice to keep drinks cool. Just think about presentation and do something different with the containers; add candy labels and birthday stickers and such to the serving bins. And be sure to keep an eye on the ice—if it starts to melt, pour some of the water out and add more ice to keep everything cool and refreshing.

Acrylic serving platters and glasses are the best bet for any outdoor function. Every size, color, and shape imaginable are available in both high-end and low-end options, and any will do the job. Clear pieces are the most versatile and can easily be brightened up with splashes of color, ribbons, or whatever else you can think of. Just, please, no more paper plates and plastic cups! Acrylic will save you money in the long run, as it is reusable and better for the environment.

Activities

We went retro for some afternoon fun by dividing the guests into teams for a little friendly competition. To build the teams we drew names out of a hat; each team member wore a T-shirt in the corresponding team color. Once everyone had formed their alliances, it was time to begin the battle!

GAMES

Limbo   Apple bobbing
Potato sack races   Dance-off
Musical chairs   Twister
Simon says   Concentration

GAME PLAY

The rules for game play were as follows:
1. Each player competes twice

2. Winner of each individual game receives a predetermined amount of points (for example, ten or fifty points for each win)

3. Team with the most points at the end wins a huge gift basket

Gift Bags

We made sure guests could relive their sugar highs by passing out clear canisters from Dylan's Candy Bar filled with Hershey's Kisses. But absolutely anything sugar related will be appreciated.

Steal It!

It's simple to create a gift bag for this party. Just fill a basket, canister, or bag with an assortment of old-school candies like Abba-Zabbas, Pop Rocks, Pixy Stix, Ring Pops, and candy necklaces. You can go to one of those candy stores at the local mall or a specialty candy store like Dylan's Candy Bar, order online, ask your guests to bring their favorite dessert or treat, or just hit the candy aisle at your local grocery store and stock up.

The Menu

We looked cavities and calories in the eye and said "Who cares?" We had a huge selection of treats, including Lara Shriftman's favorite chocolate-coconut cake, cherry pie from the Beverly Hills Hotel, and Serena's pièce de résistance: carrot cake. Carnival carts served up snow cones and cotton candy in addition to tons of traditional candies.

Candy: Swedish Fish, Sour Patch Kids, Chiclets, Ring Pops, candy necklaces, Red Hots, Pop Rocks

Old-School Snacks: Pink Sno-Balls, Ding Dongs, Twinkies, Hostess cupcakes

Krispy Kreme doughnuts

Pink flower cookies from Cookies by Design

Chocolate-covered pretzels, toffee, and **popcorn** from Peterbrooke Chocolatier

Cupcakes and caramel marshmallows from Joan's on Third

Chocolate-coconut cake and **cherry pie** from the Beverly Hills Hotel

German chocolate cake from Jerry's Deli

Carrot cake from the Ivy

Assorted brownies and cookies from Mrs. Beasley's, and Miss Grace lemon cakes

Frozen treats:
Otter Pops, pints of Ben & Jerry's ice cream, and Cold Stone Creamery ice cream

Equipment
Food carts from Barts Carts
Cotton candy cart
Snow-cone machine
Ice-cream truck
Novelty ice-cream cart filled with fruit bars, ice-cream sandwiches, and drumsticks

> **CHIC TIP**
> *I'M MELTING, I'M MELTING!* BE CAREFUL WHEN SERVING FROZEN TREATS; LEAVE THEM OUT FOR ONLY A SHORT PERIOD OF TIME OR HAVE THEM PASSED AROUND ON TRAYS.

Drinks

At our party fun, fruity concoctions were garnished with candy and passed on trays sprinkled with candy. Whatever you serve, don't forget to have tons of water and nonalcoholic options, especially if the party is held outside. People get very dehydrated (and sugar tends to make you thirsty), so gather an assortment of thirst quenchers.

Frozen strawberry margaritas

Snow cones made with tequila

Arnold Palmers (part iced tea and part lemonade)

Lemonade ice cubes in star shapes

Soft drinks: Coke, Diet Coke, Sprite

Bottled water

What better way to cure a sweet tooth than with candy from Dylan's Candy Bar and ice cream!

Sitars &
Samosas
The Perfect Indian Fête

Guests mix and mingle under the stars at this open-air cocktail and dinner party.

Ask an
expert!

Once you've de-
cided on a theme,
don't hesitate to turn
to someone well
versed in the cul-
ture. We consulted
our good friend Dr.
Raj Kanodia, who
routinely throws
authentic Indian
dinners. He gave us
tons of recommen-
dations, which
included hiring the
chef from his
favorite LA restau-
rant, the Bombay
Café; setting up a
tandoori oven; and
having dancers for
entertainment. If
you don't have an
expert on speed
dial, get inspired by
visiting a store that
sells Indian goods,
browse the Internet,
or pick up a book.
Note the colors,
flowers, and music
and let your imagi-
nation take over.

P**eople love to attend parties** where the décor is out of the ordi-nary, and any ethnic theme, from a Mexican fiesta to an Asian dim sum party, immediately puts guests in a festive mood. Exotic decora-tions and authentic food can turn the evening into a minivacation.

The event we threw to celebrate Cheryl Howard's first novel, *In the Face of Jinn,* is the perfect template for planning your own Indian dinner. We organized an amazing fête on the grounds of Brian and Gigi Grazer's home. The Grazers hosted the event along-side Renée Zellweger and Henry and Stacey Winkler. More than 150 guests began arriving at 7:00 p.m., and they spent the evening enveloped by Indian traditions, including tandoori cooking and performances by sitar players and Indian dancers.

Every detail whisked the guests off to another land, from the antique Bangladeshi furniture to the deeply colored Pakistani fabrics. The expansive backyard was tented and seamlessly divided into a variety of spaces, including a bar, a dining area, and a couch-filled den.

No matter what kind of budget you have, this party is very easy to re-create at home. The most important element in any ethnic-themed event is food, but once you've decided on how to whet your guests' taste buds, go the whole nine yards and satiate every other sense.

Adding cultural touches like dancers and musicians to your party is a must. But please, don't bore your guests with a long recital. You don't want the performance to take up the bulk of the evening or it breaks up the flow. Remember, they came to a party, not a show! To create the feeling of being at a bazaar in Bangladesh, we had dancers and sitar players circulate among the guests and perform in small groups throughout the evening. A perfect balancing act!

CHIC TIP
ORDERING TAKEOUT—MEXICAN, INDIAN, CHINESE, ITALIAN, WHAT-EVER YOUR TASTE BUDS DESIRE—IS ALSO A GREAT OPTION FOR AN ETHNIC DINNER PARTY, ESPE-CIALLY IF YOU'VE INVIT-ED A SMALL GROUP. JUST DON'T LEAVE THE FOOD IN TO-GO CONTAIN-ERS: MAKE A BEAUTIFUL PRESENTATION BY ARRANGING THE FOOD IN COLORFUL BOWLS AND ON PLATTERS.

Guests got in the mood during dinner with a performance by the Taal Dance Troupe, while tabla, djembe, and majari musicians circulated through the crowd.

Location

Select a location that guests will be curious to see, whether it's a museum or someone's home; a unique setting adds allure to your event. Another budget saver is to throw the party at your favorite ethnic restaurant—the décor is already in place. But keep in mind that throwing an event at a private residence makes the night more personal and intimate. It also allows guests to get a peek at a place they may otherwise never see. In our case, guests were very excited to see the Grazers' large estate. It lent an exclusive and elegant tone to the night, and the natural surroundings were the ideal backdrop.

After selecting your location, identify any difficulties guests may have upon arrival. Is there ample parking? Will guests have to walk a long distance? The Grazers' driveway is quite long and is situated in the hills, so both parking and distance needed to be addressed. After all, you don't want your high-heeled guests arriving sweaty after trekking to the party. We rented golf carts to transport everyone to the party entrance, and to keep the ambiance festive, we lined the driveway with luminarias. If you can't afford to rent golf carts, enlist the neighbor's teenaged son and his friends to help with valet parking. Just be sure that your guests are well taken care of so that this night is one to remember.

CHIC TIPS

WHEN THROWING A PARTY AT A PRIVATE RESIDENCE WHERE THE HOST DOESN'T WANT PEOPLE INSIDE THE HOME OR IN A CERTAIN AREA OF THE RESIDENCE, SIMPLY LOCK THE DOORS, BLOCK OFF THE ENTRANCE WITH A VELVET ROPE, OR HIRE SOMEONE TO MAN THE DOORS.

KEEP GUESTS ENTERTAINED AT THE END OF THE NIGHT BY HAVING THE VALETS HAND OUT ROSES, OR HAVE COFFEE AND TEA AVAILABLE WHILE GUESTS WAIT FOR THEIR CAR.

Toss vibrant-colored throw pillows in all shapes and sizes on couches and chairs. Create additional (and inexpensive) sitting spaces with ottomans and over-sized square pillows.

Flowers

Flowers are a key part of the decorating for an Indian-type fête. We filled concrete vessels with water and floated gardenias and orchid blooms. In the tent, a primitive container with brightly colored florals created an exquisite focal point. Silk-wrapped floral arrangements served as center-pieces at the dining tables, while blossoms were scattered across all the other tabletops, from the bar to the coffee tables. Decorate with blossoms native to India, like champac, Indian jasmine, and plumeria.

Steal It!

If you're making a floating arrangement, Dr. Raj recommends earthen bowls that keep with the Indian theme.

Flowers are always wonderful to string into leis and drape throughout the room.

Add blossoms to serving platters and dinner plates for a pop of color against the food.

CHIC TIP
PUT DOWN THE PLASTIC! INSTEAD OF BUYING OR RENTING, SAVE MONEY AND BORROW ITEMS FROM FRIENDS. ONLY PURCHASE ITEMS THAT WILL WORK FOR OTHER PARTIES OR IN YOUR HOME.

The Playlist

Dr. Raj recommends mixing Indian beats with hip-hop tunes for a worldly mood. His favorite artists are Rishi Rich, DJ Satnam, and DJ Taj. In a dinner party setting like this, keep in mind that you want the music to be upbeat and lively, but still in the background so guests can easily converse.

If you want more of a vibrant atmosphere, have the music ebb and flow through the evening. Start off with cool, smooth tunes and then slowly rev it up with more energetic songs as the night goes on. When you want the party to end, wind down with some mellow music.

Décor

Instead of going to the regular party rental company for basic tables and chairs, we rented ornate furniture such as etched side tables and carved benches and ornamental decorations such as Buddha busts from import and antiques stores. Since we had a large backyard, we were able to create different settings and areas for the guests to explore.

The main area featured a richly colored dining space, with pumpkin-, curry-, and topaz-colored linens over tabletops and buffets. Nearby, a maharaja tent was set up as an intimate conversation space, with rattan chairs, ottomans, floor pillows, and thick sisal rugs to cover the grass. Since cocktail service should always be easily accessible, a long bar was placed in the middle. Off to one side, an ornate screen provided a backdrop for the book signing, and a string chaise longue held copies of the book. Other small groupings of couches with coffee tables were nestled under trees to create the feeling of private courtyards.

Steal It!

Look for items that match your theme's décor, like vibrant throw pillows, engraved coffee tables, and intricate wood-carved furniture.

Create a homey area to lounge on by covering the ground with sisal and Indian-print rugs.

Fill the space with warm, vibrant colors. Look for amber, topaz, curry-yellow, brick-red, and turquoise fabrics. Contrast these hues with batik prints and embroidered materials. Mix, match, and loosely arrange the materials on the buffet, dining tables, couches, and chairs.

Create an area with loungelike vignettes either under a rented tent or under a big shade tree. Create additional (and inexpensive) sitting spaces by placing big square pillows around a coffee table.

To keep the look elegant, florist
Eric Buterbaugh recommends
abiding by this golden rule: less is
more. Just a few gardenias floating in an earthen bowl are perfect

Party Highlight: Guests were having so much fun, the party lasted three hours longer than planned! Make your party a success by designing a cozy space. For example, we placed space heaters in the lounging den and cocktail areas to keep everyone warm when the night grew chilly.

Jackie Collins's tip for throwing a book party
"Keep it moving. Be sure to always have your book in your hand for photo opportunities. And call all of your celeb friends to guarantee great PR."

Peter Som's clothing tip for an Indian theme party
"Wear jewel tones with gold accents. Remember, a little goes a long way. If you want to deal with a full sari the whole night, be prepared."

WHO WAS THERE 1. Henry and Stacey Winkler, and Cheryl and Ron Howard **2.** Greg Lauren and Elizabeth Berkley **3.** Ellen DeGeneres and Portia de Rossi **4.** Renée Zellweger and Lara Shriftman **5.** Lara Flynn Boyle **6.** John Carrabino and Renée Zellweger **7.** Elizabeth Harrison and Iran Issa Khan **8.** Jason Bateman and Chris Kattan **9.** Ron Howard and George Lucas

Invitations

We wanted this invite to stand out among the batches of bills and magazines that fill the mailbox. We sent out a single-panel invite with party information and a single graphic on the front panel, while the back panel was handmade and had a deep claret henna design. We slid the invite inside an intricate die-cut envelope. It was so beautiful that guests couldn't wait to open it!

Steal It!

Choose an Indian-inspired paper color such as rich orange or deep yellow.

Select a postcard or image, like the Taj Mahal or a group of Indian women, and photocopy it. Or simply attach the picture directly to the card stock.

Go classic with Cartier Smythson or Tiffany stationery or any other thick card stock. Use an Indian-inspired font and print out the invite in a deep red color. Attach the invite to Reed's ginger candy.

Serve It!

Though it was a proper dinner, we didn't assign place settings. Instead we served the meal buffet-style and allowed guests to choose their own tables. This kept the vibe loose and casual despite the elegant setting.

Hire waitstaff to help serve food and ensure that the buffet is fully stocked during dinner.

Ethnic menus are not made up of ordinary American food! It's imperative that the staff is educated about the dishes and their ingredients.

Dress servers and all waitstaff in traditional attire, like saris and tunics.

Cover the buffet tables with an assortment of rich fabrics in different colors and textures.

Serve It!

Select ornate platters that have a unique shape, color, or design. Dress up plain white or silver platters with brightly colored flowers, flat colored marbles, or swatches of printed material. Accoutrements that add both texture and color to the tray, leaves, flower petals, and rocks are all great options.

And don't forget to add elements to the bar top as well. Look for amber, topaz, curry yellow, brick red, and turquoise fabrics. Contrast these hues with batik prints and embroidered materials. Mix, match, and loosely arrange the materials on surfaces where you are serving the drinks and food.

Lighting

Lighting is incredibly important, especially at an outdoor party. We lined the driveway with candles, hung lanterns, and positioned spotlights on the ground to light up the trees. And, of course, candles of every size and shape were placed on all the tables.

Steal It!

Buy votive candles and lanterns that look Indian-inspired.

Create a dramatic look by lighting trees at the bottom so that the light filters up through the branches.

For warmer lighting, place colored gels in amber tones over bright spotlights.

String white Christmas lights in the trees and around buildings. No matter what time of year it is, the twinkling adds an instant festive feel to the environment.

Music

The eclectic Alien Chatter Band, a musical group that fuses classic ethnic tones with modern funk, provided the night's music. In addition, the roaming sitar, tabla, djembe, and manjari musicians provided a lilting backdrop to the setting. If you plan to have any sort of live music at a dinner party like this, be sure to give it a natural feel by placing the musicians in various spots around the venue. Place colorful throw rugs on the ground and light the area with votive candles.

If you can't afford live music, simply play an Indian-inspired soundtrack or pick up a copy of Alien Chatter's CD. At the end of the evening, hand out copies of the music to all the guests so they can re-create the evening anytime!

Gift Bags

Instead of handing an official gift bag to guests upon their exit, we set up a gifting area where all guests could try on Delman shoes. Cheryl Howard gave away signed copies of her novel, *In the Face of Jinn*.

Steal It!

Hand out bags of Indian candies or set up bowls of candy such as White Rabbit sweets and Gavinda's ginger candies near the exit for guests to reach into on their way out.

Fill a colorful bag with a bunch of Indian-inspired goodies like a carved-wood picture frame, a jasmine- or sandalwood-scented candle, incense, and a recipe for one of the dishes served during the evening.

Create a CD with music that reminds guests of the evening or give them a copy of a funky CD, like Alien Chatter's.

India brings to mind sensual, floral experiences, which we carried through to our bar service. Add a scented touch to cocktails by floating an edible flower (we used nasturtiums in our punch), or hang a playful elephant charm on the glass. And don't forget to have your servers wear authentic garb. It's these types of finishing touches that truly make a theme party work.

Vanilla-gingersnap Grey Goose cocktails with mango mix

Indian beer, such as Kingfisher

Strawberry-nectar tropical punch

Chai and organic coffee

The Menu

The menu is the centerpiece of an ethnic-themed party, so it was incredibly important that we serve authentic Indian recipes. Luckily, we had Los Angeles's renowned Bombay Café on hand to create the perfect feast. We started the evening with an assortment of appetizers set out on serving stations or passed around on trays and then moved on to a huge buffet-style dinner that included traditional vegetarian and meat dishes. A tandoori oven was set up on the premises for baking naan and the delicate Chilean sea bass. If you want to hold an ethnic-themed party on a lower budget, bringing home takeout is the perfect solution. Just head to a great ethnic restaurant and order up your favorites.

APPETIZERS

Lentil-and-rice pappadams with assorted chutneys

Assorted raw vegetables with walnut chutney

Vegetable samosas with tamarind chutney

Miniature potato pancakes

Sev puri (diced onion, potatoes, noodles, chutney, and cilantro on bite-sized wafers)

DINNER BUFFET

Chicken masala

Tandoori Chilean sea bass

Indian farmer's cheese-spinach puree

Basmati rice with cumin seeds

Yellow moong dahl with fried onions

Cauliflower with turmeric

Eggplant deva

Plain naan

Mango chutney

Tray-passed Dessert

Petit fours with a sunburst design

CHIC TIP
SOME LIKE IT HOT, OTHERS DON'T! WHEN SERVING ANY SORT OF ETHNIC OR EXOTIC MENU, ALWAYS INCLUDE A FEW SIMPLE AND RECOGNIZABLE ITEMS FOR THOSE WITH LESS ADVENTUROUS TASTE BUDS.

Make it colorful! Cover the buffet tables with an assortment of rich fabrics in different colors and textures.

Afternoon Splash
Sun & Fun, Poolside

Sunning by the pool in terry-cloth-covered chaise longues—what a perfect way to spend a summer afternoon!

LOOSE JUICY BEACH

Inspiration for a party can come from anywhere; in our case, working on our suntans gave us the idea for our afternoon splash. If you're having a hard time coming up with a fresh approach, take time to relax and think about the things you love to do, the places where you feel the most content. Now take those ideas and apply them to your fête. It's that simple!

"GUESTS DON'T WANT TO SEE THEIR HOST STRESSED OUT AND RUNNING AROUND. REMEMBER, AT A CERTAIN POINT YOU NEED TO LET GO AND LET THE PARTY TAKE ITS COURSE."
—ALEXANDRA VON FURSTENBERG

N othing says it's summer like a **pool party!** Guests love casual afternoon parties because the day is sure to be easy-going and fun. For the launch of Juicy Couture Swimwear, we invited 250 guests to a sun-soaked fête inspired by "Old Hollywood." With the Beverly Hills Hotel as our inspiration, we styled the lush grounds of the Burndorf Estate in a colorful array of pink, green, and white.

While the mood was laid-back, the setting was light and luxuriant with white terry-cloth chaise longues and plenty of grouped seating. We created a perfect space for everyone to kick back: Shade-seeking guests lounged in wispy curtained cabanas, sun lovers basked on chaise longues grouped by the pool, while athletic types like Michelle Rodriguez hit the tennis court.

The focal point of the afternoon was a fashion show featuring the new swim line by Juicy Couture, with the hilarious Sandra Bernhard as emcee. A white runway was constructed around the edge of the pool so the models could strut with the sparkling water as the backdrop.

Whether you plan to throw a poolside bash for friends or to launch a product line, as we did, it's simple to re-create this party. Just channel your inner Marilyn Monroe, and get ready to splish and splash!

Every girl loves to play dress-up!

Enlist your daughter, niece, or neighbor girl and have her wrangle her friends together for a "fashion show." An older sibling can play the emcee role or play great tunes so everyone gets involved. The girls can create outfits from their own closets or a thrift shop, or they can ask a local boutique to help out. Better yet, make the show a bitch 'n' swap. Girls can model their own outfits and then trade them with their girlfriends. After the show, the girls can trade clothes and add a new twist to their closet.

A model sports the latest looks in the Juicy Couture swim line.

Location

In this case, the party was all about the location. The Burndorf Estate provided an amazing setting, with its pristine pool and lush grounds, but to throw a casual afternoon party, you don't have to have an elegant mansion. There are a ton of options that will work just as well.

Steal It!

Park it! We love to take over a patch of Central Park and invite our friends out for a casual afternoon outing.

Check out the local Y and see if it has a pool for public use.

Make some calls to local hotels and see if they have a poolside spot available for reservation, or even an after-noon rental. Remember, off days like most weekdays will be more affordable than a Saturday afternoon around a major holiday!

Borrow a friend's or family member's backyard pool.

Find a sandy space at a local beach or lake. Check in ahead of time with park officials to find out whether you need to reserve a fire pit, picnic table, or gazebo and whether or not alcoholic beverages are allowed on the grounds.

> **CHIC TIP**
> LOOKING TO GET MORE FLOWERS FOR YOUR CASH? HEAD TO YOUR LOCAL FLOWER MART AT THE END OF THE DAY WHEN VENDORS SLASH THEIR PRICES.

A panoramic view of the Burndorf Estate.

Flowers

Beautiful pink and white flowers with greenery adorned the side tables around the vignettes, while taller arrangements graced the bar. White orchids, hydrangeas, and pink baby spray roses, mixed with large shiny anthurium leaves, are all great choices for these type of arrangements. If you decide to add different-colored blossoms, don't mix the hues themselves; instead, create contrast by setting single-colored arrangements near one another.

We were careful to vary the size and shape of all of our arrangements to add balance and movement to the setting. Don't just scatter the flowers throughout the space, but create interesting groupings; sets of three, or any collection of uneven numbers, are the perfect choice, as they are more exciting to the eye.

The Playlist

The DJ kept the crowd in the summertime mood. In a steamy setting, it's important to have upbeat music, but don't turn it up too loud. Keep the tunes at a volume that allows the guests to converse without yelling (leave the thumping bass for nightclub parties!).

Cruel Summer
Bananarama

California Dreamin
Mamas and the Papas

Going Back to Cali
LL Cool J

Strict Machine
Goldfrapp

Trick Me
Kelis

Girls on Film
Duran Duran

Wicked Little Girls
Esthero

Décor

A large main canopy tent created a breezy and shady spot where the guests could mingle. This square-shaped open space was perfect because people could spot their friends and keep an eye on all the action. In addition, private cabanas were placed throughout the yard and around the pool and piled with pink towels and pillows embroidered with "P&G" (the initials of Juicy designers Pamela Levy and Gela) and "Choose Juicy."

All the furniture, including chaise longues and daybeds, were grouped together in cozy vignettes of four to six and eight to ten to create conversation spots. Plant stands spray painted pink served as end tables and provided a space for people to place drinks and food, while wooden trays were placed on the daybeds. Remember, the key is to have plenty of comfortable seating so guests will want to hang out all afternoon!

Steal It!

Skip the usual red and blue and decorate with sunny colors, like pink and green.

Rearrange seating in vignettes of four to six, six to eight, and eight to ten. This gives guests a comfortable place to relax, mingle, and meet new people.

Bring indoor furniture outside. Give that kitchen chair or living room couch a makeover by draping it in white sheets or a playful fabric like terry cloth.

Create the ultimate lounge space by bringing out a bed and loading it up with pillows.

Use patterned rugs or large bath mats to lay a soft foundation for sitting on the ground. Prop fluffy pillows throughout the party space.

At a hardware store, purchase cut tree trunks as end tables.

Hammocks are a great addition to any pool party.

A signature Eric Buterbaugh rose bouquet was placed on mini pink picnic tables throughout the venue.

Party Highlight: When planning your guest list, strive to have a cool combination of people; don't invite just the same old group of friends. Add to the core group by asking your friends to help with the guest list. People want to meet new people at parties, so branch out: Invite your doctor, coworkers, and even that new guy you met last week. We had such an amazing mix of people that our party went well into the evening!

WHAT'S YOUR BEST PARTY TIP?

"Plenty of booze. Some kind of game or activity for people to participate in. Karaoke—always a crowd pleaser." — **David Arquette**

"I like parties that are outside or in someone's house. Good music—by that I mean music I like. Parties with people that I have fun with." — **Luke Wilson**

"Have parties at home with people you really enjoy. Don't do it for the sake of having a party." — **Billy Bob Thornton**

WHO WAS THERE 1. Stephen Dorff and David Arquette **2.** Lara Flynn Boyle and Selma Blair **3.** Serena and Venus Williams with Luke Wilson **4.** Reggie Miller and Maria Menounos **5.** Brittany Murphy and Nicole Richie **6.** Jennifer Love Hewitt **7.** Denise Richards **8.** Models showing off a bathing suit fit for a bride **9.** Kate Beckinsale and daughter **10.** Fergie and Macy Gray

Invitations

We made a splash by sending out green kickboards with the invite printed on the front. To set the Old Hollywood mood, we chose a font reminiscent of the Beverly Hills Hotel's font and its signature palm-tree logo. The kickboards were wrapped in pink tissue paper and packaged in a pink box featuring address labels printed to match the invitation.

CHIC TIP
ALWAYS CREATE A PERSONALIZED INVITE! E-MAILING AN INVITATION MAY SEEM LIKE A QUICK FIX, BUT A CUSTOMIZED INVITATION MAKES A GREAT IMPRESSION.

Steal It!

Keep the invite clean and cohesive by using the same font and colors everywhere, from the packaging to the labels.

Create miniature kickboards by using white poster board or foam core cut in the shape of a kickboard. Then print the invite directly onto a piece of pink or green card stock from a computer or handwrite the invite using a green pen, and attach to the poster board or foam core.

Buy one size of pink paper (five by seven inches) and another size of green paper (four by six inches). Print the invite on the smaller, green piece of paper and create a border by attaching it to the larger, pink paper.

Scan Old Hollywood images from a postcard or book. Or purchase thematic stickers like palm trees and sandals to affix to the paper invite.

Attach the invite to something that says "pool party," like a pair of flip-flops or a bottle of suntan oil, or print out the invite on a bathing cap or small terry-cloth towel.

Serve It!

Don't skimp on hiring help; extra hands will make the day more enjoyable for you! Check with the waitstaff at a local restaurant and find out which servers are available the day of your party. Be sure to give them a dress code; for example, we dressed our serving staff in pink Juicy collared shirts and white shorts.

While we prefer passing hors d'oeuvres around on trays, you can serve them buffet-style. Just be sure all the items can sit outside.

Always place buckets filled with bottled water, cold beer, and iced tea around the grounds so guests can help themselves. If you're not going to hire a bartender, save yourself time: Make the cocktails before the party and refrigerate them.

Flowers

Pink mesh vases filled with flowers of different heights were placed in odd-numbered groupings throughout the white canopy tent, on side tables and next to vignettes.

How to Wrap a Vase

Tall bouquets of bright green anthuriums and pink baby roses arranged in a fabric-wrapped vase added a delicate touch to the ambience.

1. **Choose a stretchy fabric** that complements your décor. Any material with a sparkle is great for an afternoon event because it catches the sunlight.

2. **Measure your vase** and then cut fabric appropriately. *Tip:* Use a piece of brown florist's paper or any thin paper to make the measurements exact.

3. **Sew** the fabric inside out to keep the seam hidden on the inside of the covering.

4. **Slip the covering** snug over the vase and make sure it's secure.

Small bouquets in short glass vases gave off a subtle pink hue.

The key to creating this arrangement is to choose two vases in the exact same shape—one that is large, and a smaller one that fits neatly inside the other.

1. **Cover the interior vase** with a swatch of fabric. You can either sew a sleeve or get crazy with the glue gun.

2. **Fill the interior vase** with evenly cut flowers.

CHIC TIP
NOT A SEAMSTRESS? WHIP OUT YOUR GLUE GUN AND WING IT!

Gift Bags

Every guest left with a little Juicy. A hot-pink swim wrap was tucked inside a fabulous hot-pink terry cloth–covered train case with "P&G" stitched in green on the outside. In addition, guests received Juicy Couture swimsuits in pink and green and a designer head scarf.

Steal It!

It's easy to create a gift bag for this occasion. Hand out pink or green sacks lined with tissue paper and fill them with any or all of the below:

Suntan oils and after-sun lotions

Evian misting face spray

Flip-flops and beach towels

A CD with songs played during the afternoon

On warm afternoons, be sure to serve plenty of libations, and don't forget to have plenty of non-alcoholic options on hand. We served an elegant mix of everything from iced tea and pink lemonade with sugared rims to strawberry daiquiris, mint gimlets, and martinis. Guests could revive their childhood taste buds with our specially prepared strawberry Creamsicle drinks.

The Menu

The food was adapted from the Beverly Hills Hotel's renowned restaurant the Polo Lounge. Cabana boys served bite-sized appetizers and desserts on stainless-steel trays with leaves decorating the bottom. The menu items were small and easy to eat by hand but still substantial, so guests felt like they had plenty to eat. Not everything has to be overly gourmet, because many people ultimately love diner food best.

HORS D'OEUVRES

Cabana gazpacho with California vine-ripened tomatoes, Sonoma garden vegetables, and extra-virgin olive oil served in shot glasses

Chopped McCarthy salad served in a festive box with black chopsticks

Mini grilled Russian sandwiches (a layered combo of turkey, ham, Swiss cheese, coleslaw, and a smear of Russian dressing on rye)

Polo Lounge club sandwiches, roasted turkey, smoked bacon, and Swiss cheese

Mini turkey burger with grilled sweet onion and portobello mushrooms, bite-sized grilled Beverly Hills sirloin burgers and cheeseburgers with caramelized-onion marmalade and homemade ketchup

DESSERT

Always serve dessert! To satiate our guests' sweet tooth we passed around both healthy snacks like strawberries, and rich, decadent treats. As a special touch we created a special dessert in honor of the hosts: petit fours with "P&G" piped in white and green icing on top.

California stemmed strawberries dipped in either fresh lime curd or white and dark chocolate

Warm chocolate bread pudding with a wisp of crème anglais served in a white china spoon

Mini sorbet cones with lemon and passion fruit, served just like at the Beverly Hills Hotel, on a Lucite cone holder

Mini homemade ice cream cones with chocolate and vanilla ice cream

Petit key lime tartlets with raspberry garnish

Dark-chocolate brownie, topped with black walnut

Delectable desserts from Kathleen Sacchi's The Fine Art of Catering, served on a beautiful silver tray adorned with leaves and flowers.

For the Tweety Birds

A Mellow Yellow Shopping Soiree

Tweety. The original Blonde

kits

Warner Brothers'
Tweety collection
in the windows
of Kitson.

How to Make Sumptuous Serving Trays

1. Measure the circumference of a serving tray. Select an image of a theme-oriented icon and enlarge the image to fit. Laminate the image and secure it to the serving tray.

2. Choose a cool fabric, cut it to fit the tray, and lay a piece of acrylic over it to hold it in place.

3. Line clear acrylic trays with yellow duckies and place food items like deviled eggs alongside them.

4. Group a bunch of colorful veggies and place dip in a clear glass bowl in the center of the veggies.

5. Gather colored leaves and use them to decorate the bottom of trays.

Sean "Diddy" Combs's White Party is synonymous with the Fourth of July, and Oprah is famous for her black-and-white Legends Ball. Make a splash with your own signature color. Go kitschy and use the hue for every detail, including the invites, serving trays, furniture, and candles—leave no item uncolored!

We did just that at the yellow-themed shopping parties—one on each coast—we threw to celebrate Warner Brothers' exclusive Tweety Bird apparel line. The shade was everywhere, from the yellow "red carpet" to the one hundred invited guests who, naturally, were all blond for this party. (For the bold brunettes we featured a wig table where the dark-haired girls could turn their locks into fair-haired waves.) And to reintroduce the bird of the hour, a person in a larger-than-life Tweety costume greeted the guests.

To prominently feature the products, we hosted the event at two fabulous boutiques, on both the East and West Coasts. In Los Angeles, guests were treated to an evening at the celebrity-frequented shop Kitson. In New York, the event was hosted at the international store Scoop, which has more than fifteen locations, including Miami and Las Vegas.

Both the LA and New York parties were saturated in shades of yellow, from the food, drinks, and serving trays, to the flowers, napkins, and tablecloths. Even the hosts embodied the theme! In LA, blonds Kaley Cuoco, Dayna Devon, Jennie Garth, Mary Alice Haney, Rachel Hunter, Caleigh Peters, Maeve Quinlan, Brande Roderick, Lara Shriftman, and Tori Spelling greeted the guests, while in New York the flaxen-haired hosts were Tinsley Mortimer, Shoshanna Gruss, Carson Kressley, Christina Applegate, Stefani Greenfield, and Kelly Bensimon.

Just because the evening was yellow, yellow, yellow, it was far from mellow!

The Latest Trend: Boutique Parties

Get with the times—boutique parties are the new art-gallery openings! We've found that throwing a bash at a chic new store makes for a casual vibe and interesting location. It's also perfect for promoting both a store and a featured designer; for example, we threw the *Charlie's Angels* premiere party at Henri Bendel, which gave guests the chance to check out the designer's new line. In addition, we've thrown store openings at Jimmy Choo, Sergio Rossi, Louis Vuitton, Hugo Boss, Hogan, Juicy Couture Las Vegas, and Cartier. After all, partyers are natural-born shoppers! It's easy to add a charitable element by giving a portion of the shopping proceeds to a deserving organization.

CHIC TIP
DARE TO BE DIFFERENT! A SURPRISING TWIST TO A COLOR-THEMED PARTY IS TO HAVE THE HOSTESS WEAR AN OPPOSITE COLOR WHILE ALL THE GUESTS DRESS IN THE SIGNATURE SHADE.

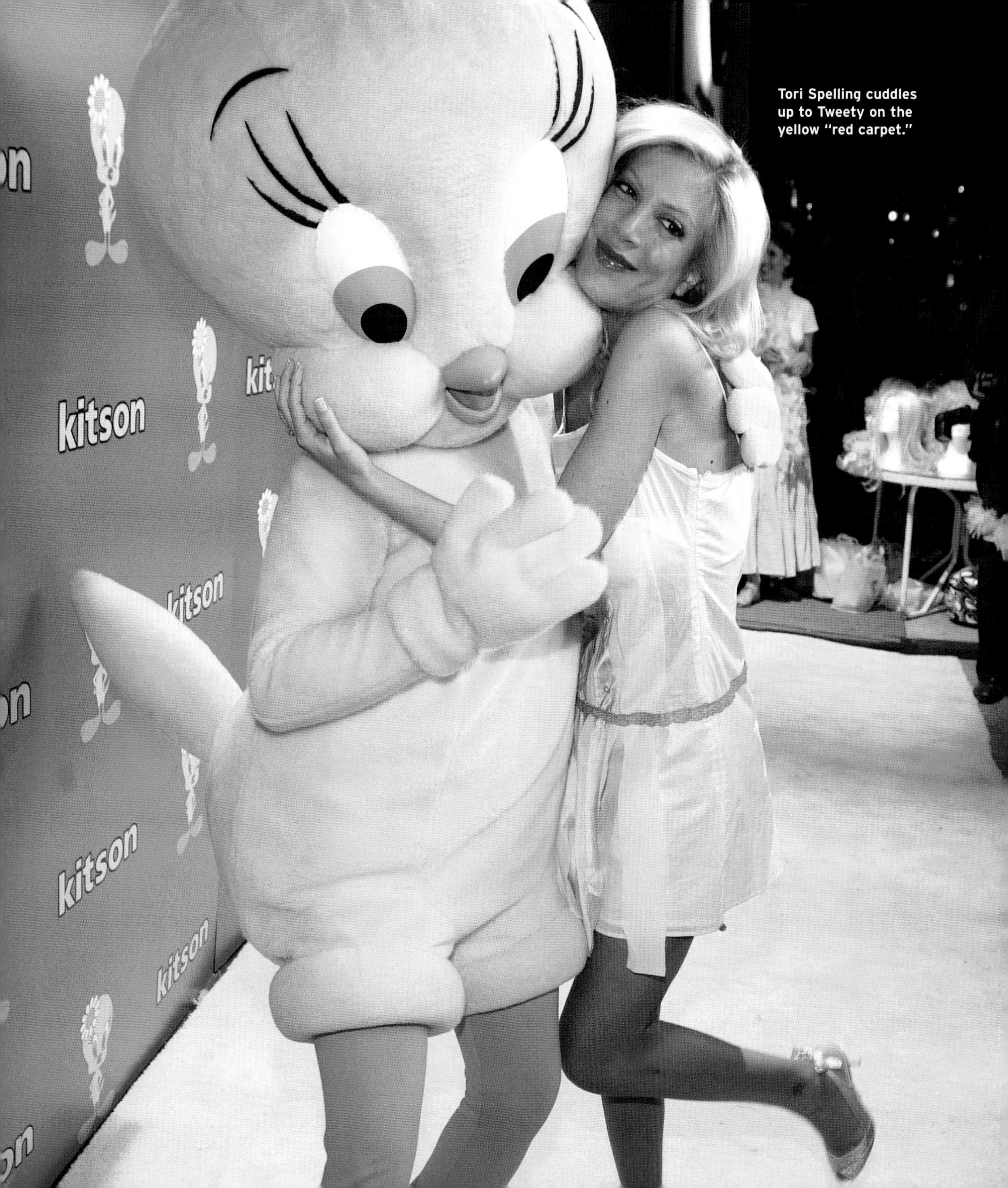

Tori Spelling cuddles up to Tweety on the yellow "red carpet."

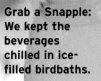

Grab a Snapple: We kept the beverages chilled in ice-filled birdbaths.

How to Create a Flower-Filled Birdbath

1. Fill a birdbath or any fabulous punch bowl with a minimum of one inch of water.

2. Snip off the stems from gerbera daisies that match your party's color and float the flowers in the birdbath. Dahlias, gardenias, and roses also look great. Just peel the petals back to balance the blossoms and keep them floating upright.

3. Candles can be added to the flowers or used alone.

4. Create a cute arrangement by placing smaller bowls filled with candles around the birdbath.

This is extremely important at a boutique location. Stores are brightly lit for shopping—not for cool ambience. You will need to either dim the lights or turn them off and use candles. If you leave the lights on, attach translucent colored cellophane paper to all the lighting fixtures to soften the glare.

Steal It!

Switch the existing store lighting to yellow-hued or rose-colored lightbulbs. To highlight merchandise or anything special to the night, shine spotlights down from the ceiling onto the products.

Place colored candles and votives throughout the room. Colored votives are simple to create. Simply wrap the outside of clear glass candleholders in colored cellophane, place a candle inside, and light!

Bring in lamps from home and cover the lampshades in fabric in the signature color. Place throughout the venue.

The Playlist

Samantha Ronson spins at the hottest parties in Los Angeles and New York. For this type of boutique party, keep the music ambient and in the background, spinning artists like Keane and Coldplay and theme-related songs.

Rockin' Robin by the Jackson Five

Fly by Hilary Duff

Fly Away (acoustic) by Lenny Kravitz

Anything by Blondie

Décor

We transformed both New York City's Scoop and Los Angeles's Kitson into club-style venues by moving displays, removing merchandise, and turning the cash register into a bar. We lighted the exterior signs in yellow and created a window display of Tweety goodies, including an exclusive Tweety-themed Vespa. Tables, including the table in the center aisle featuring food items, were covered in yellow fabric, while birdcages stuffed with Tweety Birds and yellow flowers were placed throughout the store. The merchandise was hung on two walls that were painted—what color? Yellow! A favorite feature was the wig table, featuring foam model heads wearing blond hairpieces, gerbera daisy hair clips, and yellow sunglasses.

Steal It!

Rearrange the boutique furniture to create walkways and comfortable gathering spots for guests.

Remove some of the merchandise to make room for places to add decorative details and a food island.

Go crazy with your signature color when choosing tablecloths, plates, and napkins.

Purchase birdcages from a craft store and fill them with stuffed animals, flowers, or balloons.

Tweety Birds around
a jar of Cookies by
Design cookies.

Party Highlight: We made the guests play a part in the color theme by asking them to wear something yellow. In addition, guests had a blast playing at our wig table, which was filled with blond hairpieces and cute daisy barrettes. That way everyone, even those who didn't have on the signature color, could get in the mood. Adding campy details like a wig table and a big stuffed Tweety Bird keeps guest entertained with picture taking, plus it adds a cool, kitschy vibe to the night.

Stefani Greenfield, owner of Scoop NYC, shares her best tips for throwing a boutique party.

"Make sure that there are not too many clothes out; only have enough out for ambience."

"Serve only clear beverages."

"Check sound and lighting—you want it dim but not dark."

"Clear a proper path for people to mingle so you feel like you are at a party and not a store."

WHO WAS THERE **1.** Rachel Nichols **2.** Kimberly Hefner and Quincy Jones **3.** Bijou Phillips **4.** Nicole Richie, DJ AM, and Nicky Hilton **5.** Maria Menounos **6.** Nicole Richie **7.** Maeve Quinlan and Tweety **8.** Nicky Hilton **9.** Lara Shriftman, Maria Menounos, and Lindsay Lohan

Invitations

Our invites were designed with our pal Tweety in mind. We used flat yellow card stock with embossed writing on the front. On the back, a felt Tweety added a little feathery touch, and to make it pop from the first moment, we sent the entire invite in a die-cut envelope. The envelope was folded around the invite and sealed with a label.

Steal It!

1. Buy card stock and four-panel envelopes in your party's signature color.

2. Select a fun yet simple font. Format the text to print in a vibrant shade that matches your color scheme.

3. Choose an image online that represents the theme of your party and copy it onto your invite.

4. Run the invitations through the printer and place them in an envelope.

5. Seal the envelopes with any variety of bright stickers in the signature color.

Ready, set, shop!

What do girls love more than a party? Shopping! Anytime you plan to throw an event at a boutique, check to see if salespeople will be available so guests can do more than browse. This can also be a great way to add a charitable element to your event: ask that the merchandise be discounted 15-30 percent and donate all proceeds to the charity of your choice.

Since our color-themed gathering served double duty as a product launch, we introduced partygoers to the new Tweety line, which included cashmere sweaters from Cake Couture and Raw 7; tees from And Cake, Joystick, Cosmofact, and Junk Food; jeweled tank tops from Bejeweled; Shoshanna bikinis; Havaianas sandals; and Madeline Beth's accessories. Everyone made shopping lists and later headed back to Kitson for new wardrobes!

Create Citrus Centerpieces

We placed centerpieces of clear vases filled with lemons and ferns throughout the venue. Luckily, these items are quite easy to arrange.

This type of arrangement can be adapted for any type of leafy plant—herbs like basil or sage are possibilities; and any citrus fruit, like oranges and limes, will work. Just pick a fruit that matches your theme color!

1. Select a large glass piece, a fishbowl-shaped vase, or anything with a nice round shape that will hold the fruit easily. Tip: Tall thin vases will break easily when the fruit is placed inside. Stick with wide oval pieces.

2. Arrange the fruit first, carefully fitting each piece inside the vase without pressing or pushing.

3. Fill the vase with water and begin placing the stems of the ferns or other greenery into the crevices created by the fruit.

Serve It!

Blond servers in white jeans and yellow "Natural Blonde" tees with feather boas passed food and cocktails around on white round trays with flat Tweety inserts. Other snacks were passed on clear rectangular Lucite boxes whose interiors were lined with yellow Peeps. Drinks were served along with yellow cocktail napkins printed with fun trivia items, like, "Tweety's name was Orson before he became Tweety." In addition, we filled birdbaths with ice and stocked them full of bottled drinks so guests could help themselves to cold beverages.

Steal It!

Instead of the usual cocktail napkin, create your own fabric coasters.

1. Choose a swatch of fabric that suits your theme. It can be a solid color or a playful print with flowers or little birds. Anything goes.

2. Cut coasters to the desired size using scissors with creatively shaped edges. *Et Voilà!*

Flowers

There can be neither too much, nor anything too kitschy, with this type of party—the more over-the-top, the better! We had a blast decorating with flowers and used them in every way imaginable. We floated pink gerbera daises in birdbaths (a spark of color makes the signature color stand out), attached yellow and pink daises to hair clips for girls to clip in their locks, and created gerbera hand-ties that were placed in columnar vases and stuffed in birdcages.

Steal It!

Fill a tall clear cylinder with lemons and arrange graceful branches in a floral-like manner.

Float yellow candles and flower buds in a clear glass bowl filled with yellow beads or marbles.

Scatter petals across tabletops and the bar.

Gift Bags

At our event, each guest received a stuffed Tweety Bird, a "Blondes Have More Fun" Tweety T-shirt, and a Tweety cookie from Cookies by Design. Whatever gift bag you decide upon, just make sure it goes with your theme. Find anything that exemplifies the color you've selected; for example, if your signature color is white, a bag filled with vanilla votive candles, fine stationery, a bottle of white wine, and mints would be perfect.

Steal It!

Stuff a bag in your theme color full of fun items in the same hue, like stationery, Post-it notes, pens and pencils, and a stuffed animal.

Fill a clear cellophane bag with tons of candy in your signature color. We used yellow candy like Chiclets, yellow jelly beans, and lemon drops, and tied the bag with a yellow ribbon.

Be sure to carry your color theme through to the cocktails as well. We had special drinks created, like the Puddy Tat and the Tweety. Other great touches included adding a wedge of lemon or serving old-fashioned lemonade. And don't forget to serve drinks to guests upon entry. At Harrison & Shriftman we always position servers just inside the door with trays of drinks.

The Puddy Tat: Kahlua

The Tweety: vodka

Grey Goose limoncello martini

Coppola yellow wine

Snapple lemonade

Voss water

The Menu

Shopping parties like these do not require a huge amount of food. While a bar is a definite must, avoid taking up precious space with a buffet; instead, have servers circulate among the guests with trays of food.

Rosemary-infused polenta triangles topped with chopped wild mushrooms

Yellow cherry tomatoes stuffed with crab salad

Crudités of yellow peppers and yellow pear tomatoes with artichoke dip

Deviled cage-free eggs garnished with minced chives

Mini corn dogs with yellow mustard

Mac 'n' cheese croquettes with melted Velveeta sauce

DESSERTS

Serve a plethora of playful colored cakes, and colorful candies like jelly beans; or, better yet, create customized cupcakes with a smear of buttery frosting or white icing and cover them with sprinkles that match your color scheme.

Lemon-curd tartlets

Tweety Bird pies: Chocolate pudding topped with crushed Oreos and garnished with a gummy worm, served in bright yellow gelato cups on a flat bed of wheatgrass

Twinkies placed in a circular pattern on serving trays, with a stuffed-animal Tweety in the center of each tray

Mini yellow cupcakes with fluffy lemon buttercream icing

Cookies by Design Tweety cookies

Assorted yellow candy, like Lemonheads, lemon lollipops, candy Lipstick, lemon jelly beans, peanut-butter cups, and Chiclets

Salty 'n' sweet: Deviled eggs served on a clear Lucite tray with marshmallow Peeps. A cute and different way to serve.

Party
Princess
A Kid's Birthday

Sophia and her
best friends.

Guest of Honor

When throwing a party for a guest of honor, be sure to find out what they want from the evening. They may want something small and intimate, a big party with tons of friends, or, like Sophia, a combination of both. And don't forget to make sure your birthday girl or boy plays the role of host, greeting guests and thanking them for being a part of the celebration.

A birthday is the best excuse in the world to go all out and throw a big huge bash, but it's especially important when it's a kid's big day. No one loves birthdays more than kids, so when Lara Shriftman's good friend Sophia began planning her eleventh, we knew we had to arrange something special and really amazing.

Sophia wanted to include everyone in her class and also do something special with her ten closest girl-friends. The solution? We planned two parties in one. Her day began with an indulgent girlie get-together. The girls were invited to her house, where John Barrett Salon and Shu Uemura treated everyone to hairstyling and makeup. After lunch—and tons of giggling and dancing—the pampering continued with manicures and "mocktails" at Buff Spa in Bergdorf Goodman.

They were all prettied up with a fabulous place to go: Sophia's Studio 54 Disco Party at Crobar. The girls were whisked off in a white Hummer limo at 7:00 p.m. for the big birthday celebration. The sixty guests, who included all the kids in Sophia's class at school, got the VIP treatment as they were greeted with a velvet rope and a bouncer who made sure their names were on the list.

It was nonstop fun once the party began, as the entertainment company Party Poopers got everyone involved and led the kids in games and break dancing—no wallflowers were allowed! A Krispy-Kreme-doughnut-tiered birthday cake was the icing on the evening. A party like this makes for the perfect birthday—no matter what age is being celebrated.

Krispy-Kreme-Doughnut Tower Cake

A four-tiered cake with tiers that are eighteen inches, fourteen inches, twelve inches, and eight inches will provide enough doughnuts for fifty to fifty-five people.

Customize your cake with icing designs and spun-sugar cages as well as edible flowers, ribbons, and beading. The ideas are endless!

Original glazed Krispy Kremes are our favorite doughnuts for this cake, but get creative and use any variety or combination of doughnuts. Keep in mind that since original glazed doughnuts are very light, they work best for the top tier. And always select a very lightweight cake topper!

The doughnut tower cake is also easy to assemble at home. Use any three-tiered cake platter, plastic or glass, and simply stack the doughnuts on the tiers. Drizzle the layers with colored icing and add long sparkler candles.

Make a wish! Sophia and her sister Ava blow out the sparkler candles on her four-tiered Krispy-Kreme-doughnut tower cake.

People, especially kids, love to hear tunes that they are familiar with so they can dance and sing along. For a dance party, include a mix of music styles—including hip-hop, dance, and rock—from all different eras. Line-dancing songs like "Macarena" are great for kids' parties because they encourage everyone to join in. DJ Jonathan Shriftman played all of Sophia's favorite artists and songs, including:

Beyoncé

Gwen Stefani

50 Cent

Fabolous

American Idol artists

Toxic by Britney Spears

Christina Aguilera

I Will Survive by Gloria Gaynor

Stayin' Alive by the Bee Gees

Dance songs like **Macarena, Electric Slide, Cha-Cha Slide, YMCA,** and the bird-dance song

Kids at Play

Throwing a dance party is only one out of thousands of possibilities. When deciding what kind of party to throw for your birthday girl or boy think about things they love to do. Are they into ponies? Then set up a day at the stables. Do they love to play video games? Turn the celebration into a tournament by renting or borrowing gaming consoles such as Xboxes, PlayStations, and Nintendos to set up a mini arcade.

Models for a Day: Invite all the girls over for a day of fashion. You can either arrange to visit a boutique or have all the girls bring a bunch of their favorite clothes so everyone can create funky new outfits. Have someone on hand to do hair and makeup and then have the girls put on a fashion show! End the afternoon with presents, cake, and ice cream.

All Swim: Every kid loves having a pool party, but make yours different by finding a fun theme. Decorate with marine life, turn the backyard into a beach, or have everyone "swim with the fishes" and make it a gangster-style bash! Of course, be sure to hire a lifeguard!

I'm Going to Disneyland: There's no better way to celebrate than with a day of roller-coaster rides and funnel cakes. Gather up a group and head out to Disneyland, Six Flags, Universal Studios, or any local amusement park. Enlist a family friend or another parent to help keep track of everyone.

Get Crafty: Got a budding artist on your hands? Stock up on supplies at a local art store—get everything you can think of including markers, glitter, canvas, paint, and molding clay. Set up different arts and crafts stations where the kids can get messy finger painting, tie-dying T-shirts, and creating other masterpieces.

Queen for a Day: Decorate the room like a castle and give each girl a feather boa and loads of inexpensive but flashy jewelry upon arrival. Give games a princess-style twist and play "Princess, May I" and "Pin the Shoe on the Princess." And don't forget to create a throne for the birthday girl! Adorn a special chair with feathers, ribbons, and balloons.

Spa at Home

It's simple to "spa" it at home! Create a manicure station by setting up a long table with chairs on opposite sides. Decorate each setting with finger bowls for soaking cuticles and soft terry-cloth towels to protect the table surface. Be sure to have plenty of cotton balls, nail-polish remover, bottles of nail color, and emery boards available. Hire a manicurist from your favorite salon, or gather up friends to do the filing and nail painting.

The girls get gorgeous before the big night. Hair by John Barrett Salon, makeup by Shu Uemura. Every little girl's fantasy!

Party Highlight: Party Poopers led the kids in roasting and toasting Sophia, which was absolutely adorable. Make your party special by doing something similar, whether it's having all the guests roast the honoree or having them raise a glass and give a fabulous toast. At the end of the evening, a hundred balloons were released over the dance floor. All the kids were having so much fun that no one wanted to leave!

TIPS FROM THE BIRTHDAY GIRL

"Always make things as pretty as you can make them. And make sure everyone has fun. Make sure you talk to each guest and personalize it. Be a good host and be kind to everyone, and be creative." **—Sophia Schrager**

Invitations

Sophia sent out adorable boxed invites that had a chic Studio 54 girl on the front and a cool red border of records, sunglasses, and sheet music. The time and info were printed on the front, along with the strict dress code ('70s disco!). The invitation was tucked into a red envelope and sealed with an "S" sticker. The front of the envelope was decorated with a happy-birthday stamp and cupcake stickers. Always make the invite age appropriate; even though this was a party at a nightclub, it still felt like a kid's birthday bash.

Steal It!

Purchase festive and colorful invites that match the theme of the party. For Sophia's party, we used Top Ten Chick stationery by greeting-card designer Robin Maguire.

Use a playful font and type text in all lowercase letters, using various point sizes to highlight specific items.

Liven up invites by using pink envelopes and sealing them with initials stickers—in our case, we used an "S" for Sophia.

Decorate the front of the envelope with birthday-inspired stickers and stamps, like cupcakes, stars, and so forth.

Serve It!

When ordering pizza, request that the restaurant stagger the deliveries. Have the first batch arrive at six o'clock, the next at seven o'clock, and then another at eight o'clock or on the hour as long as you want to continue serving; that way there will always be fresh, hot pizza to eat. Also request to have the pizza cut however you want it—in squares or with the slices cut in half so you can serve the pizza as an appetizer. You can make appetizers out of any fast food, such as McDonald's French fries; for instance, just leave the fries in the wrappers and have them passed around all night long.

Day of Beauty

The day of beauty was an amazing treat for Sophia and her gang of girlfriends. They were treated like celebrities, getting their makeup carefully applied and hair coifed by the professionals at Shu Uemura. Afterward, they left with a personalized gift bag filled with the perfect colors to match their complexions. What's not to love about that?

Steal It!

Everyone has a beauty pro in their circle of friends, so if you can't afford to bring in a professional group of makeup artists, barter with a pal to play stylist for a few hours.

Head to a drugstore or beauty counter and stock up on eye shadows, blushes, and lip glosses in soft colors. Don't go too bold with the hues; no one wants to come out looking like a petite version of Tammy Fay Baker!

Steal It!

Make a customized nail polish by printing labels that say "Sophia's Princess Pink" or "Sophia's Disco Red" and sticking the new label on a bottle of nail polish. Giving the gift a personal touch is a fun reminder of the day.

Take a makeup bag and customize it for each guest by making labels that say something like "Lara's Makeup Stash" and then fill it with lip glosses, blushes, and eye shadow.

Remember, it doesn't have to be anything fancy—just make it relate to the birthday party!

Gift Bags

For a fun keepsake from the evening, the kids had their pictures taken with cardboard cutout figures like Austin Powers, Dr. Evil, and Marilyn Monroe. At the end of the evening, the pictures were printed out and glued onto matching bobblehead dolls.

Steal It!

Anything fun will do for the kids. Hand out bags of candy, cool games, and photo keepsakes from the evening.

While the girls got their nails done at Buff Spa in Bergdorf Goodman, they felt like stars as they sipped nonalcoholic drinks from fancy champagne flutes.

Nonalcoholic green-apple martinis

Capri Sun

Kool-Aid Burst tropical punch in punch bowls, with star-shaped ice cubes

The Menu

For the girls' afternoon, we wanted to keep it very casual. We served a ton of munchies, like grilled cheese, hamburgers, and a variety of potato chips, buffet-style so the girls could serve themselves. Pushing the chairs away from the dining-room table created an open setting, while the colorful serving platters and bowls served as decorations.

Above all, a children's birthday party should be simple. We had very little decoration other than a beautiful flower bouquet that Sophia received from Stephen Dorff.

GIRLS' LUNCHEON

Pop Burgers: Serve these in their original boxes and place packets of mustard, ketchup, and mayo in clear bowls so the kids can dress their burgers themselves

French fries

Grilled cheese and peanut butter and jelly, cut in triangles with the crusts cut off and stacked neatly. Dress up sandwiches for a special occasion with gourmet cheeses, peanut-butter spread, and raspberry preserves

Pigs in a blanket

Pretzels, Lay's potato chips, and Cheetos, served in acrylic bowls in assorted colors

Miniature candies, like Snickers or SweeTarts

DANCE PARTY

The food was served completely casually, just the way kids like it. Pizza was delivered, cut into squares, and served straight from the pizza box. We stacked paper plates and napkins next to the food so the kids could eat with their hands and then continue dancing and playing. We also passed around lots of candy treats tucked in votive glasses.

Pizza from Two Boots, cut into squares

Krispy-Kreme-doughnut tower made from thirteen dozen doughnuts and drizzled with blue icing, with eleven extra-long candles

Sugar cookies featuring photographs of Sophia and her sister Ava

Votive candleholders were set on trays and filled with tons of green and sour-apple-flavored candies like Willy Wonka Laffy Taffy and apple Jolly Ranchers

CHIC TIP
ADD A PERSONALIZED TOUCH TO A BIRTHDAY OR ANNIVERSARY PARTY BY SERVING COOKIES DECORATED WITH PHOTOGRAPHS OF THE GUEST OF HONOR. CHOOSE YOUR FAVORITE PICTURES. WE CHOSE THE ONE OF SOPHIA AND HER SISTER AVA DOING BACKBENDS.

For a kid's party, it's great to have drinks set out in buckets with ice, in addition to having them passed around on trays. Kids love to grab a drink like a Capri Sun, suck it down, and then get back into the action. Just be creative with how you arrange the beverages—use fabulous buckets and containers in different colors, shapes, and sizes.

Easy-to-eat, classic kids' favorites served buffet-style around the dining-room table.

Let the Fur Fly!
A Party for a Dog's Best Friend

Hosts Mr. Guinness, Sam, and Greta Garbo pose with Maeve Quinlan and Lara Shriftman, with Lara Flynn Boyle and her dog Lilly, and Ross and Kelly of Kelly's Pet Care.

Fun on Four Legs

Since this day was all about pampering the guests' canine kids, we featured dog-friendly services like grooming and "peticures." We've included great ideas to make your dog day a success.

Bow-Wow Babysitter

If you're having more than a few dogs and especially if they haven't interacted before, it's helpful to have a professional dog-care service on hand. Kelly's Pet Care routinely takes between twenty and thirty animals to the dog park, so they easily kept the situation under control at our party.

E ven if you're not an animal owner, you've probably been invited to a wedding joining Rover and Fifi or an afternoon barbecue celebrating Lulu's second birthday. Animal lovers know no bounds when it comes to their four-legged kids, and, being pet lovers ourselves, we decided it was time to throw a stylish doggy do in honor of our furry friends.

We invited twenty-four celebrity guests and their pets for a playdate starting at 2:00 p.m. at Ryan Drexler's Malibu home. *Celebrity Living* magazine joined paws with furry hosts Sam, Mr. Guinness, and Greta Garbo for this casual afternoon affair fêting the dog days of summer.

We took our cue from the posh pet boutique Fifi & Romeo and decorated the outdoor area in black and white, with miniature-poodle stuffed animals as centerpieces. We also made our guests part of the color scheme by asking them to don their summer whites.

With the help of Kelly's Pet Care, the parents relaxed by the pool while their canine kids wrestled and tumbled in the gravel-coated backyard. In addition we had an acupuncturist and psychic on hand—for the dogs, of course. This is such a great twist on an afternoon party and a perfect way to spice up an expected gathering. Suddenly your afternoon goes from a weekend barbecue to a day with the dogs!

A Woofy World

These days it's easy to treat your four-legged pal like a celebrity. At the W Hotels they do everything short of rolling out a red carpet. Fido gets his very own welcome basket filled with toys and treats, and he can even order room service off the doggy menu.

And your pup can look like a star with designer leashes, collars, and tags from Hermès, Gucci, and Victoria's Secret's doggie-inspired line, PINK, which also boasts cute stuff for mom! Target even showed off its dog clothing during New York's Fashion Week. Now that's a pampered pup!

> "ALWAYS THANK YOUR HOST."
> — SARAH MICHELLE GELLAR

Kimberly Stewart
with her dogs
Bently and Bliss.

Doggy Menu

Don't forget to have plenty of treats for the dogs; after all, this is their day. We had an incredible spread from the Three Dog Bakery, which specializes in goodies for dogs. Just be sure to keep the puppy chow away from the people grub so no one accidentally munches on a Beagle Bagel. We served all of the dog treats on silver platters from Tiffany & Co.

Pup cakes: sweet wheat-flour cupcakes with doggy frosting

Pup tarts: sweet dog treats with a flaky shell

Beagle Bagels: crunchy sweet bagel chips with a carob-chip swirl

Ciao-Wow Cheese Pizza: garlic dough topped with low-fat Parmesan, oregano, and garlic

Dottie's Dipped Delights: peanut-butter dog bones dipped in carob

Dino Bone: dog bones dipped in carob

Harlequin hearts: heart-shaped cookies dipped in carob

Sarah's Slab O'rrr RRRibs: garlic-dough bread in a light honey sauce

SnickerPoodles: cinnamon cookies

Celebration Cake: apple-cinnamon cake with carob chips and peanut butter

Beastro Biscotti: cinnamon dog biscotti with peanuts

Three Dog Bakery doggy treats nestled on a classic Tiffany serving tray.

Lazy Dog Day

Don't forget, even dogs need a place to relax. Fifi & Romeo set up a cozy spot for the played-out mutts to kick back and chill—or at least chew on some stuffed animals. We carried the black-and-white theme through to this area and filled it with all kinds of fun stuff from the boutique, including big, puffy beds and a little dog-house—because you never know when that barking someone will need a time-out!

To make the spot shady and cool, we created a tent by draping white curtains over rods that were embedded in the ground for stability. Stuffed animals and toys decorated the lounge so guests like Greta and LuLu could sleep, play, or just relax.

> **CHIC TIP**
> CREATE A LOUNGE SPOT WITH OLD PILLOWS AND SOFT BLANKETS, OR ASK PET OWNERS TO BRING OVER EXTRA DOG BEDS.

The Playlist

DJ Shrifty put the "dog" in "dog party" by playing canine-themed songs from his iPod. Remember, during afternoon parties such as this one, it's important to keep the music in the background so people can talk; plus, loud music can be frightening to dogs!

Who Let the Dogs Out by the Baha Men

Who Am I? (What's My Name?) by Snoop Dogg

Call Me a Dog by Temple of the Dog

My Best Friend by Bad Dog No Biscuit

Hey Little Doggie by Kool Songs

I Love My Doggy by Steve Sargenti

Hound Dog by Elvis Presley

A Hard Day's Night by the Beatles

Décor

Who let the dogs in? We did! To make room for the party animals, we moved the pool furniture off to the side, but we made sure we still had plenty of chaise longues set up so that the human guests could lie out. In addition, dog beds were set up as spots where lazy dogs could chill, while fluffy white pillows created a place for the two-legged guests to relax. We also sectioned off the courtyard and created a space where the dogs could play while the people food was served.

The black-and-white color scheme was inspired by the posh LA pet boutique Fifi & Romeo. We covered two sets of tables in black-and-white fabric, and the serving staff was outfitted in the boutique's staff uniforms. The guests were asked to dress in white, so they also participated in the decoration. Miniature-poodle stuffed animals were used as centerpieces, along with floral arrangements from Eric Buterbaugh. In addition, as with any outdoor party, we filled baskets with H$_2$O Plus Oasis Mist face misting spray and Alba Organics sun-care products.

Steal It!

If the tables don't match, head to a fabric store and purchase bolts of fabric. Any mix and match of colors and patterns will do, including black fabric with a polka-dot overlay, white fabric with a striped overlay, and so on.

Trim the fabric to fit the tables.

Pick out fun center-pieces, like miniature-poodle stuffed animals, or dog chew toys.

Fifi & Romeo
set up a doggy
boutique.

Party Highlight: Since it's a dog-day afternoon, send guests home with a keepsake that reminds them of the event, whether it's a bottle of "Pawlish" for the dog or a cute framed photo taken during the gathering. We had staff circulate throughout the party with digital cameras to take photos of guests with their pups and printed the photos right there.

WHAT'S YOUR BEST PARTY ADVICE?

"Whatever you wear, don't have your dog wear a matching outfit."   —**Peter Som**

"Invite a mix of great people."   —**Allison Sarofim**

"Relax and have a great time yourself, and so will the guests."   —**Alana Stewart**

"As a hostess, you must introduce people and throw out something they have in common."   —**Maeve Quinlan and Jennifer Finnigan**

"Be sure you're not monopolizing the conversation." —**Michael Kors**

WHO WAS THERE 1. Yana Syrkin and Owen Swabe from Fifi & Romeo **2.** Alana Stewart and Pimp Juice **3.** Lara Morgenson and Freddy **4.** Lara Shriftman and Greta Garbo **5.** Lara Flynn Boyle **6.** Mary Alice Haney and Leroy **7.** Lara Flynn Boyle and Jonathan Shriftman **8.** Chloe Davenport and Stella **9.** Jennifer Finnigan and Saucisson **10.** Casey Johnson with Zoe and Gracie, and Nicky Hilton with Beau

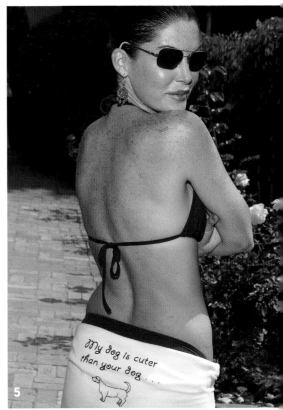

Invitations

We wanted to get the point across from the moment our invited guests saw the invitation, so we filled clear jars with bones purchased from the grocery store. All the essential details were printed out on a piece of paper that we tied to the jar with a bow. Any size or type of container will do for this invitation; just keep in mind that it needs to be hand-delivered or carefully packed so the bones don't break!

Steal It!

Take a sheet of white, polka-dot, or black paper and place a piece of sheer vellum on top. Punch a hole at the top and tie the pieces together with a ribbon. Fold the invitations and place them inside mini-envelopes. Be sure to match the invitation colors to your party theme.

Decorate the card stock and envelope with dog stickers.

Take a picture of yourself and your dog and use the photo as part of the invitation. Print or handwrite the party details around the photo.

Serve It!

To keep the color theme prominent, we served the food in a variety of black-and-white serving platters, dipping bowls, and baskets. Create a pleasing arrangement by mixing a variety of shapes, sizes, and colors. For example, line a large square black serving tray with individual-sized clear glass bowls.

> **CHIC TIP**
> BE CREATIVE WITH SERVING TRAYS AND TRY TO THINK OUTSIDE THE BOX. OR, AS WE DID, JUST USE THE BOX. (FOR EXAMPLE, WE USED FIFI & ROMEO GIFT BOXES AS SERVING TRAYS.) SIMPLY LINE THE TOP OF A BOX WITH TINFOIL, COVER THE TINFOIL WITH A NAPKIN, AND SERVE UP THE GRUB.

Steal It!

Serve grilled pita bread on black-and-white Fred Segal serving platters, and the hummus dip in individual-sized black bowls.

Arrange individual-sized square glass dishes of steamed rice on a large black-and-white serving tray.

Pile garden vegetables in a black three-tiered basket.

Serve Greek peasant salad in black paper cups on a white serving tray.

Line a wrought-iron basket with tinfoil and white napkins and fill it with chicken kebabs and jumbo shrimp.

Wrap fries in a black-and-white polka-dot gift bag and tie the bag with a pink ribbon.

Fur Maintenance

Send the dogs home freshly bathed!
Playdates often leave dogs dirty and
smelly, so we treated our guests to
hot-oil treatments by TLC Mobile Pet
Grooming Service.

**"Peticures"! Give 'em the star treat-
ment!** OPI nail technicians pampered
the pets' toes with OPI's nail "pawlish." If
you can't hire actual manicurists, create
your own salon by setting up a table with
pet-friendly nail polish.

Sun Savers

How many times have you rushed off to
a barbecue or pool party, only to get
there and realize you forgot to apply sunscreen? At every afternoon event we
throw, we always provide plenty of sunscreen because no one wants to go home
with a nasty burn or unsightly tan lines!

Steal It!

Don't pull out old, grimy bottles of
sunscreen. Blech! Make the lotions look
appealing by stocking up at a drugstore
on a variety of brands and SPFs.

Pick out a container that looks good
with your décor and fill it with bottles
and misting sprays.

If it's an exceptionally warm day,
create soothing compresses by soaking
washcloths in cold water and a touch of
lavender oil. Keep the cloths invitingly cold
by submerging them in buckets of ice, and
place them next to the sun worshippers.

Gift Bags

Talk about a lucky dog, each canine got a
bag filled with gifts—but they had to
share some of the goodies with their
owners! We filled a polka-dot bag with
pink polka-dot dog outfits; treats from the
Three Dog Bakery; and tons of stuff from
Fifi & Romeo, including a handkerchief, a
handmade sterling-silver charm tag,
a hand-patched cashmere scarf with a
matching pet sweater, a hand-knitted
wool sweater, a cashmere beanie, and
a dog bowl. Plus, the owners took home
Victoria's Secret Pink pj's and sweatsuits—
perfect for those early morning walks! We
also tossed in a CD specially made for the
day, full of dog-inspired tunes.

Steal It!

**Create a bag filled with a bunch of fun
items** like dog bones, a dog cleaning
brush, and leashes and collars.

**Snap photos of guests with their
dogs** and hand out framed shots.

To satiate the dogs' thirst, we placed water bowls throughout the venue, while the owners sipped on a variety of frozen cocktails. In addition, we placed buckets filled with ice, bottled water, Snapple, and Corona beer in various spots so guests could help themselves.

Bloody Mary

Frozen margaritas

Bottled water

Miller, Budweiser, and Corona beer

CHIC TIP
ALWAYS SERVE DRINKS IN ACRYLIC GLASSES AT OUTDOOR PARTIES TO AVOID ANY UNWANTED ACCIDENTS, ESPECIALLY WITH DOGS RUNNING AROUND. IN ADDITION TO HAVING SERVERS CIRCULATE WITH TRAYS OF DRINKS, PLACE PLENTY OF WHITE ENAMEL BUCKETS FILLED WITH ICE-COLD BEVERAGES THROUGHOUT THE SPACE.

The Menu

You can do any kind of food for a dog party, for example, barbecue or sandwiches, but we had a favorite Malibu eatery, Taverna Tony, cater the event. The Greek-style munchies were both passed around and arranged on large platters that were set up buffet-style so guests could serve themselves.

Grilled pita bread: homemade fresh pita, grilled to perfection

Hummus dip: chickpeas, tahini, garlic, and lemon

Greek peasant salad: crisp lettuce, tomatoes, cucumbers, onions, bell peppers, spring onions, feta, and olives, served with secret-recipe dressing

Chicken-breast souvlaki (skinless, boneless kebabs): tender cubes of chicken flavored with a hint of garlic, oregano, and lemon

Jumbo shrimp served Taverna-style in rich tomato sauce with garlic, spring onions, fresh herbs, and feta

Taverna fries: homemade Greek-style fries sprinkled with kefalotiri cheese, oregano, and pepper

Sides of steamed rice and garden vegetables

DESSERT

The desserts took inspiration from the honored guests, naturally! We served fun treats like bone-shaped chocolate bars from Romolo Chocolates, filled decorative dog bowls with bite-sized candies, and stuffed tons of cookies in jars. Remember, chocolate is toxic to dogs, so be sure your guests don't feed chocolate candy to their pets, even if it looks like a dog treat!

Good Humor ice-cream bars on silver trays

Romolo Chocolates gourmet puppy chow, served in individual miniature, decorative dog bowls

Dreyer's Dibs ice-cream treats, served in black bowls

Cookie jars with an assortment of cookies such as Oreo, biscotti, chocolate dog bones from Romolo Chocolates, and fresh-baked Nestlé Toll House chocolate-chip cookies

Small portions of eclectic Greek delicacies from Taverna Tony were served to guests.

Serious and amateur
poker players
gathered at the
W Hotel Los Angeles
for a night of
blinds and bluffs.

Poker Party
Boys' Night Out

Wanna be a high roller? Our tournament director, the renowned Annie Duke, showed guests how to bluff like a pro. With a ton of accolades under her belt, namely winning $2 million in the No-Limit Texas Hold 'em World Series of Poker Tournament of Champions, Duke knows her stuff. She's coached celebrities Ben Affleck and Matt Damon and shared her story in the book *How I Raised, Folded, Bluffed, Flirted, Cursed, and Won Millions at the World Series of Poker.*

CHIC TIP
A POKER PARTY CAN ALSO PERFORM DOUBLE-DUTY AS A CHARITY EVENT. SIMPLY SELECT A WORTHY CAUSE OR HAVE EACH PLAYER SELECT ONE THAT IS NEAR AND DEAR TO THEIR HEART, AND THEN DONATE THE FINAL POT. THIS WAY EVERYONE WINS.

Poker is a chic source of entertainment and everyone from the Hollywood hunk to the desperate housewife is bellying up to the card table. Best of all, this activity can easily be the basis for a full-blown party, a casual night with friends, or just an excuse for a weekly get-together.

We invited forty card sharks to the W Hotel Los Angeles for a night of poker and lessons with pro poker champ Annie Duke. Out by the pool we created a game area for serious players and plush lounge areas for the social butterflies. In the hotel cabanas we offered relaxing treatments like hand massages, tarot card readings, a cigar bar, and a huge dessert buffet.

When gathering a guest list for poker night, invite people who are either avid players or interested in learning to play. Don't stress if everyone isn't the best of buds; we quickly found out at our party that a shared hobby brings people together—especially card games.

It's easy to dress up this traditional guy's night out, whether you're in the mood for a high-end poker evening or a casual night of cards. Poker Night doesn't have to be for boys only. You can make it a coed mixer like ours—just remember to throw in a little something for the girls, like a manicurist. The ideas in this chapter can be applied to any kind of game night—Monopoly, Cranium, Clue—or add it as an element to another fête like a birthday, anniversary, or bachelor party. All bets are on!

Annie Duke's Top 5 Beginner Poker Tips

1. Fold more often than not. In a ten-handed game you should be playing only about 20% of the hands you are dealt. Stick with hands that have an Ace and a face card or pairs that are 55% and better.

2. Play aggressively. When calling, you only win if you have the best hand. By raising you can win if you have the best hand and if your opponent folds.

3. Be aware of position. Sitting to the left of the dealer means you act after the other players. This is a huge advantage because you know what all the other players have done before you make your decision.

4. Read every book and watch all the DVDs you can get your hands on. There is a wealth of information available and much of it is presented by the best players in the world. Take advantage!

5. Watch every hand that is played at the table, even when you fold. Keeping a close eye on your opponents' moves enables you to pick up on their patterns so when you play a hand against them later, you'll recognize their moves.

If you can't have a poker star like Annie Duke at your table, go for the next best thing and pop in her DVD, *Annie Duke's Advanced Texas Hold 'em Secrets: How to Beat the Big Boys*. Cheryl Hines demonstrates her poker skills as she deals a hand.

Party Flow

Timing is everything when throwing a party and it's especially important when the night revolves around a game. Though the card play is the focal point of the party, we wanted to create a relaxed and fun vibe so our guests didn't feel rushed. We stationed servers with Lucky Lady green martinis right by the door and began circulating appetizers so guests were encouraged to mingle for the first hour. During this time everyone signed up at a table for their level of play, beginning, intermediate, and advanced.

In the second hour tournament host Annie Duke gathered everyone together and announced the stakes. Players broke up into tables while the rest of the guests kicked back in the W Hotel's cabanas (our chic version of the loser's lounge) where they indulged in spa services and hung out at the cigar bar.

After the first round of play, the winners from each of the three tables meet at the Winner's Table for the final round. The night concluded with the last man standing receiving a huge gift bag and a moment to bask in the limelight!

How to Set Up a Poker Blind

A poker party can last an hour or all night long depending on how you set up the blinds. Blinds are forced bets made by the first two players to the left of the dealer. Usually a four-hour tournament is ideal for a party atmosphere, but keep in mind that predicting when a poker tournament will end is far from an exact science. Wild games could end quickly with players busting out or slower if people play tight. Following these tips will help you somewhat schedule the evening.

1. If you want your tourney to last about four hours, set each blind for twenty minutes then raise them; thirty-minute or longer blinds will extend the play to six hours or more.

2. The first big blind (or the first hand dealt) should be around 1/50 to 1/25 of the initial buy in. So if you start with one thousand chips, the first blind should be between twenty and forty chips. The final big blind can be the same as your starting chip amount or a few levels higher. We started our tournament at $2,000 and ended with a big blind of $10,000.

3. After setting the starting and ending blind, fill in the middle with gradual increases. Keep the first two or three levels low to encourage new players to learn without losing big.

4. Each big blind should be twice as large as the previous big blind. The small blind is usually one-half or two-thirds of the big blind.

Annie Duke's Top Five Poker Party Tips

Whether you invite five or fifty players, Annie Duke shares her top five tips.

1. Set the initial buy in at an amount that people can afford to lose. You need to play for some money so that the chips have meaning or the game isn't any fun.

2. Invest in all-plastic playing cards. Most cards are paper cards coated in plastic that fall apart and get ratty after only one night's use. Plastic cards are a little more expensive but worth the investment. You can even run them through a washing machine and they won't get ruined!

3. Make sure you have a good poker table, a poker tabletop that can be set on your kitchen table, or—at the minimum—a piece of felt to throw over the table. Without felt, it is very difficult to pick up chips and cards, plus the gaming pieces slide everywhere. Felt makes for a much smoother poker game.

4. Serve all drinks in low, wide-mouthed glasses. Beverages are easily knocked over as people reach for chips and pots, so having a glass with a low center of gravity will help prevent accidents.

5. Keep it clean! Don't serve greasy or messy finger foods, and that includes potato chips. As the player's fingers become oily, so do the playing cards and poker chips and that leads to a big greasy mess.

Remember, whether you throw your party at a chic spot or at home, always include a cozy area where both the "losers" and nonplayers can kick back.

1. **Pick out a tray you like.** It can be square, rectangular, round; silver, gold, or red.

2. **Line up enough votive candleholders** to completely cover the tray bottom. Use the same shape for the tray and votive holders; we used a square tray filled with square votives. The holders either can be all the same or varying heights.

3. **Gather the three design elements:** flowers, cut glass (which can be purchased at any flower mart or hobby store), and tea lights or votive candles.

4. **Cut the stems off the flowers** and place in the bottom of the votives. We used orchids but any simple bloom like roses or tulips will work as well.

5. **Add water until it covers the blossoms.** Obviously, do not add water to the candles unless you are using ones that float.

6. **Alternate the blossoms with the cut glass** and candles throughout the tray in an organized, yet haphazard manner. Leave some votives with just the glass, others with glass and candles, and some with a single blossom. Continue until all the votives are filled.

The Playlist

Keep the music in the background during any kind of game night. If you've got serious gamblers on hand, you can choose to have no sound in the game room (so catchy song verses don't interrupt the thought process). Play something mellow in the lounge area or where the nonplayers are hanging out. Cuban sounds or light jazz is a great choice. If you want more of a vibrant atmosphere, start off with cool, smooth tunes and then slowly rev it up with more energetic songs as the night grows later.

Décor

The W Hotel Los Angeles provided the perfect setting for our high-end poker tourney. The space included the pool area with five candlelit cabanas where we set up fabulous indulgences, including massage and pedicure treatments from Bliss Spa, astrological consultations, and a fantastic cigar bar complete with poker chip lighters. Plus, for the card novice we also had a cabana where the guys from The Poker Room gave poker lessons.

To create a resortlike respite for guests and poker players, we placed W Hotel pool beds and extra-deep sofas and lounge chairs in tight groupings and piled them with pillows. Bottle service was set up on the side and center tables of each vignette so guests also had the choice of serving themselves.

In the game area we splurged on handmade Italian poker tables from New York's The Poker Room. This luxury game shop specializes in creating unique, finely crafted game tables that are made to order.

Steal It!

Create a poker table by placing green felt, which can be purchased at any hobby shop, fabric store, or online outlet, over a large round table. Be sure players will have enough elbow room; if it looks crowded, then add another table.

Borrow poker tables or poker tabletop sets from friends or rent from a local game store.

Mix and match pieces of furniture from different rooms to create a cozy, clubby corner where players can retreat after losing out.

Rent a gaming console such as Nintendo that offers a video poker game.

Set up a cozy area with a television for nonplayers to gather and watch a favorite TV show or DVD.

One thing you can definitely bet on is that people will go crazy over dessert at any and every party. We dedicated an entire cabana to the sugar lovers and filled it with everything from poker chip cupcakes to ice-cream sundaes.

Party Highlight: Who doesn't love a winner? If you're playing for charity or a small amount of money, it makes the evening more eventful by giving out a winner's prize. We presented the poker champ with a gorgeous prize package that included a two-night stay at W Hotel Times Square, a fabulous Grey Goose martini set, the Corzo Tequila VIP kit, and the Nintendo DS system with the World Championship Poker: Deluxe Series game. The prize doesn't have to be big and splashy: It can also simply be a gift certificate or a copy of Annie Duke's book.

WHO WAS THERE 1. Anthony Anderson, Cheryl Hines, Richard Kind **2.** Marly Shelton **3**. Annie Duke **4.** Ricardo Chavira, Camryn Manheim, Richard Burgi **5.** Beau Flynn and Camryn Manheim **6.** Elizabeth Harrison, Mark Moses, Ricardo Chavira

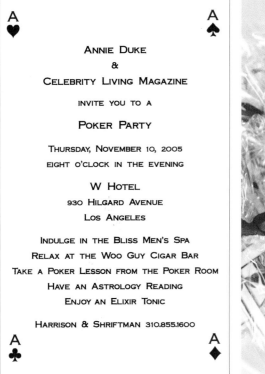

A♥   A♠

ANNIE DUKE
&
CELEBRITY LIVING MAGAZINE

INVITE YOU TO A

POKER PARTY

THURSDAY, NOVEMBER 10, 2005
EIGHT O'CLOCK IN THE EVENING

W HOTEL
930 HILGARD AVENUE
LOS ANGELES

INDULGE IN THE BLISS MEN'S SPA
RELAX AT THE WOO GUY CIGAR BAR
TAKE A POKER LESSON FROM THE POKER ROOM
HAVE AN ASTROLOGY READING
ENJOY AN ELIXIR TONIC

HARRISON & SHRIFTMAN 310.855.1600

A♣   A♦

Invitations

Our invite was a chip off the block, literally. Guests were hand-delivered poker sets from The Poker Room along with a classic invitation printed from Cartier. There are tons of fun ideas to get your guests in the gaming mood, from sending a game set to creating homemade invites.

Steal It!

Copy a classic poker image—it could be a full house, pair of aces, dice, or poker chips—onto a piece of stationery. Go classic with white or get playful and choose a green color reminiscent of gaming felt.

Place handmade invites into an oversized envelope with a few poker chips.

Print the invite on a sticker and place it on a poker chip, an oversized die, or a deck of playing cards.

Serve It!

Most people think poker night goes hand-in-hand with bowls of mixed nuts, a bag of pretzels, and greasy pizza. The W Hotel's Nine Thirty Restaurant catered a menu of chic, easy-to-handle finger foods. Each dish was served in small bite-size pieces, like a spoonful of salad in a wedge of endive lettuce or lobster soup in a demitasse cup. To keep the menu feeling fresh, we served a new item every hour.

And we added a Las Vegas touch by having servers dressed as '40s cigar-girls who circulated with drinks, cigars, and trays of candy.

When guests begin arriving, have servers at the entrance with trays of drinks and appetizers.

How to Set Up Bottle Service

1. Place a bottle of quality vodka like Grey Goose in an ice bucket and center it on the table. If your surface is soft like an ottoman, arrange everything on a serving tray.

2. Arrange highball glasses around the bucket.

3. Fill multiple carafes with soda water, tonic, orange juice, and cranberry juice. Set alongside tumblers and vodka. It's also chic to include cans of energy drinks like Red Bull along with the mixers.

How to Make a Poker Serving Tray

1. Choose a serving platter and measure its dimensions.

2. Find a poker image that you like and have it blown up to the dimensions of your serving tray.

3. Laminate the enlarged image to avoid ruining it and place it on the bottom of your serving tray.

Lighting

Candlelight is inexpensive and an absolute must-have for every party, even on game night. Of course, when playing poker or any game, it's imperative that the players can see their cards, so always keep the game room brightly lit. But you still want to create ambience in other areas of the party, so go for flickering light in the lounge area and any entryways.

At the W Hotel, the pathway from the entrance to the outdoor pool area was lined with candles, the cabanas were filled with pillared candles, and floating in the pool was a square Lucite tray bearing flaming torches. On the side tables we placed a combination of square glass votives filled with tea lights intermingled with orchid blossoms.

Steal It!

Line pathways and stairways with either votive candles or luminarias (paper sacks filled with sand and tea lights).

Replace regular lightbulbs with softly hued pink or amber bulbs throughout the household.

Place a scented candle in the bathroom.

Light the lounge area with tons of candles in different shapes and sizes.

> **CHIC TIP**
> CREATE A GAME NIGHT VASE BY ATTACHING PLAYING CARDS TO A CLEAR GLASS VASE. FILL WITH MONOCHROMATIC FLOWERS OR DROP IN A TEA LIGHT AND USE AS A CANDLEHOLDER.

Gift Bags

Guests came away with a W Hotel canvas bag stuffed with Bliss Spa products, Annie Duke's Poker DVD, WooGuy Cigar and Smoke Shop cigars, The Poker Room's poker chips and deck of cards, Corzo Tequila, Grey Goose Vodka Shaker, and poker-themed note cards from Cartier.

Steal It!

Playing cards

Chocolate poker chip coins

Lottery tickets — always the parting gift to gamble on!

The Menu

The W Hotel's California chic restaurant Nine Thirty, which serves delicious organic and farm-raised foods, catered the evening.

Beef Carpaccio Pizza with Caramelized Figs, Shaved Pecorino, Arugula, and Truffle Oil

Spinach, Dungeness Crab, and Artichoke Dip

French Fries with Three Dipping Sauces: Romesco Aioli, Malt Vinegar Aioli, and House Made Ketchup

Asian Chicken Salad with Sesame Vinaigrette and Fried Wontons

Sweet Corn Soup with Lobster Oil and Lemon Mascarpone

Shrimp Cocktail with Curry Aioli and Cocktail Sauce

Seasonal **Ciao Bella Sorbets**

Steal It!

If you can't afford to have the night catered, get kitschy with the menu. Serve homey items that people love to eat, like pizza or to-die-for French fries from your favorite place. If possible, arrange to have them delivered throughout the evening so you always have a hot batch. Serve them just like they do at the restaurant in paper containers, or buy small paper cones and add a special dipping sauce.

How to Make a Drink Menu at Home:

1. When serving specialty drinks, it's incredibly helpful to have a drink menu on hand so guests can mull over their choices and order the one that sounds delicious to them.

2. Create a drink menu from the same paper used for the invites. We used Robin Maguire's paper trimmed in red and black, so pick anything that either goes with your color scheme or the theme of poker.

3. Type descriptions of the drinks you plan to serve in the same font used for the invites.

4. Print out as many menus as you need—one, five, or ten—and head to a copy store to laminate each card.

5. Set the menus out at the bar or wherever you are serving up the drinks!

> **CHIC TIP**
> NIL THE SPILLS! GLASSES TEND TO GET KNOCKED OVER WHEN PLAYERS REACH FOR A WINNING POT, SO PLACE SIDE TABLES NEXT TO PLAYERS TO HOLD THEIR DRINKS.

Drinks

At the beginning of the evening, we stationed girls from the W Hotel's famed club Whiskey Blue at the doorway with trays of its signature drink, the Green Lady Lucky Martini. The girls continued to circulate throughout the party and took orders from the players during the poker tourney. The Whiskey Blue bartenders (dressed up in hunky black tuxedos) mixed up specialty drinks named after poker hands. In addition, we set up mini bars in each of the cabanas so people could make their own drinks.

The cabanas also boasted a Corzo Tequila bar and Elixir Teas & Tonics bar while Grey Goose Vodka bottle service was placed at each vignette.

Executive chef Travis Lett created an amazing menu by taking a bit of California cool and mixing it with indulgent treats people love to eat.

Live trees are great for framing the room and bring a fresh, outdoorsy feeling to the space. It was the perfect addition to our Malibu-inspired book party.

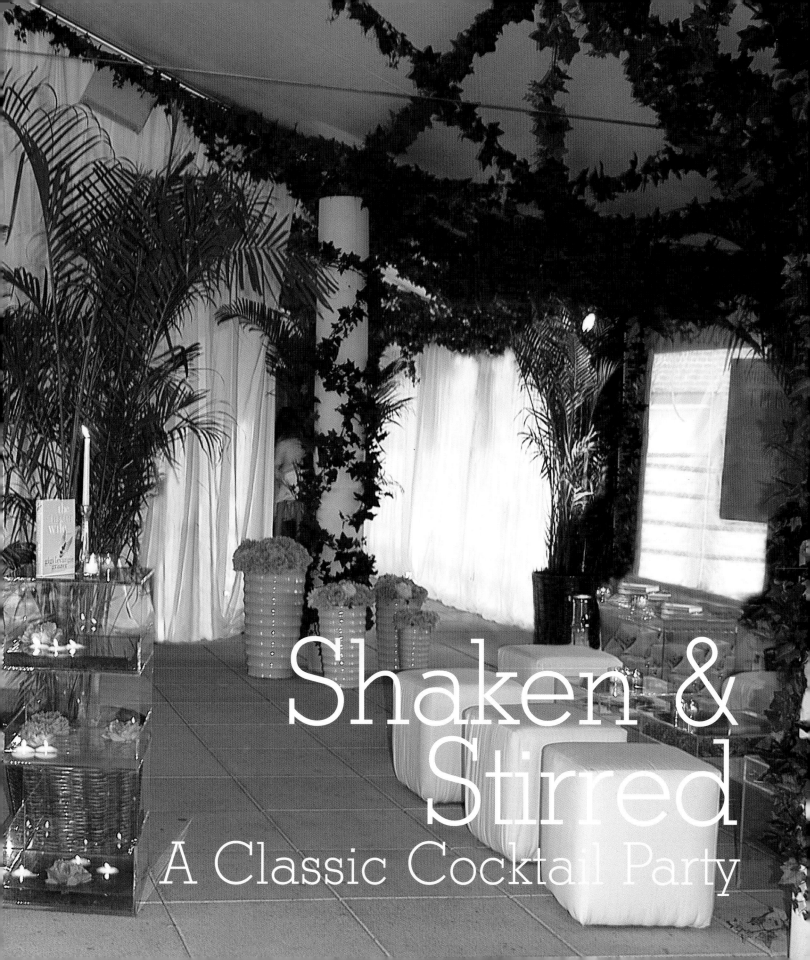

Shaken &
Stirred

A Classic Cocktail Party

Whether you're hosting a gathering of friends or celebrating a birthday, the classic cocktail party is always a fabulous fête. One of the key elements is location—the swankier the better. Of course, throwing a cocktail party in your home is always acceptable, but it's definitely hotter in a new and unexpected space, such as a cool hotel suite or the private room of a classic restaurant. For the launch of Gigi Grazer's novel *The Starter Wife*, we threw two parties. First we held a splashy event at the Beverly Hills Hotel's Polo Lounge, in Los Angeles, and then we re-created the concept in a posh penthouse at New York's Hudson Hotel.

Though this evening was a book party, it was hardly a business function. Both Gigi and her book are witty, fun, and light, and we wanted the party to reflect her personality. We asked her closest friends, Susan Campos, Angela Janklow, and Julia Sorkin, to host the event for some two hundred guests in LA, while in New York, Les Moonves, Rita Schrager, and Brian Grazer hosted the party.

We created a setting inspired by her novel, which takes place in Malibu and follows a forty-year-old divorcée reeling after her husband leaves her for Britney Spears. Elements from the book, such as the cover image of a pink lady toting a suitcase, the must-have Malibu fashion of UGG boots, and chapter quotes, became a part of the décor at both parties.

Whatever the occasion, whether it's a book signing or a class reunion, the classic cocktail party is an old favorite that easily becomes a chic new treat.

Party On!

A cocktail party is a fabulous and informal way to entertain. Make it simple and serve wine and cheese, or caviar and Cristal Champagne, but keep in mind your party's time frame, because that's what sets the mood. Traditional cocktail hours are from 5–7:00 p.m. or 6–8:00 p.m., so the one-bite rule is in effect. Serve nibbles like shrimp cocktail, chips 'n' dips, and cheese and crackers. For anything after 9:00 p.m., opt for a combo of salty 'n' sweet, with an emphasis on dessert. Cocktail hours are easy on the partygoers, and they make for a pressure-free situation. Guests can drop by on their way to dinner, turn in early, or make it a preparty stop before an all-night affair.

The bars dazzled with diamond-studded vases arranged with pink roses that glittered with a diamond center. Make your own by adding sparkling crystals to flower buds. It's inexpensive and just as fabulous!

Location

Suite Dreams. At Harrison & Shriftman, we believe that location is everything, especially when we are throwing a cocktail party. The space helps set the vibe and should go with the time of the party. For example, our LA party was an early-evening outing that began at 6:00 p.m. Nothing fit this mood better than The Beverly Hills Hotel's Polo Lounge. This setting was a huge draw because of its Old Hollywood history and celebrity clientele. Just the thought of sipping a drink where Marlene Dietrich dined is enough to make some folks feel like stars themselves, and that added panache to our party.

On the flip side, if you're leaning toward a late-night function with a hip, urban feel, then a trendy city hotel is ideal. Our New York party was in a posh penthouse at the Hudson Hotel. The incredible views of the Hudson River and Manhattan gave the night a chic vibe. There's nothing more glam than quaffing classic cocktails while looking out at an amazing skyline.

CHIC TIP
ALWAYS ARRIVE AT LEAST FORTY-FIVE MINUTES EARLY TO ENSURE THAT EVERYTHING IS SET UP AND LOOKS ABSOLUTELY PERFECT. IN THE EVENT THAT THINGS ARE NOT ARRANGED AS PLANNED, THIS SHOULD GIVE YOU TIME TO MAKE LAST-MINUTE ALTERATIONS.

Create ambience by placing votive and pillar candles throughout the room — and they serve as an alternate source of lighting that will flatter everyone.

Lighting

We kept the mood soft and ambient by placing rosy colored gels over wall sconces, on the uplights, and in the ceiling lighting. A '30s brushed-nickel chandelier added a decadent touch to the book-signing canopy and softly lit the lush greenery and hot-pink bougainvillea that covers the grounds of the Beverly Hills Hotel.

Steal It!

Create luminous pink hues by replacing regular lightbulbs with rose-colored bulbs. Alternate methods include covering white lights with a pink lighting gel or purchasing glass filters from a local lighting store.

Head to a hardware store and buy dimmers to use with floor lamps.

Get things glowing with loads of candles. Float them in clear Lucite trays filled with water, and place votives everywhere.

CHIC TIP
THERE'S A REASON IT'S CALLED THE *GREAT* OUTDOORS, SO WHEN WEATHER PERMITS, ALWAYS HAVE AN OUTSIDE AREA. AN OPEN-AIR SPACE GIVES WILD THINGS A PLACE TO COOL DOWN AND GIVES SMOKERS A PLACE TO LIGHT UP.

Playlist

We opted to spin tunes that highlighted the Malibu vibe of Gigi's book. DJ Samantha Ronson spun frolicking tunes from the Beach Boys and Marvin Gaye, and even made a CD for guests to bring home. Other accompaniments to a classic cocktail party include suave and sultry tunes from **Cole Porter, Ella Fitzgerald, Elton John,** and **Burt Bacharach.** If you're not a musical savant, **Pottery Barn** always sells great mixes.

Décor

Don't like the color scheme of the place you rented? No problem; it's simple to create your own blank slate. In both New York and Los Angeles, we did an extreme makeover of our spaces. We decorated with sheer pink fabric and draped the entire room—from floor to ceiling—in white chiffon. We covered the rug with a thin light-pink carpet, brought in modern white furniture, and added clear Lucite side tables filled with peonies. Personal touches like Yahoo! personals ads for all of the male characters in *The Starter Wife*, and quotes from the book, were hung over the existing artwork, and a square white mobile bookshelf held copies of Grazer's book.

Steal It!

Hide existing artwork and wall color by hanging sheer fabric from the ceiling to the floor. This creates a blank canvas for your decorating scheme.

Add simple accents like silk dupioni pillows in a variety of shades.

If furniture is not provided, bring in chairs, tables, and couches from home or from a rental place and cover them in white fabric. Create tight groupings by snuggling couches and chairs close together.

Use a variety of tables, including Lucite trunks filled with flowers or anything colorful; create side tables by layering white high-gloss paint on unfinished wood pieces; and cover any other incidental tables with white fabric.

Measure the floor space and then purchase a carpet remnant. Cut it down to the proper size to cover the existing floor, then tack the corners down with gaffer's tape (available at any hardware store).

Scatter plush sheepskin rugs or fluffy white bath mats in front of couches, chairs, and ottomans.

Amazing floral creations in Lucite holders were surrounded by rose-colored glass candles and pink peonies. These were placed on clear trunks stuffed with UGG purses that were handed out as parting gifts at the end of the evening.

Party Highlight: Indulge your guests' inner Paris Hilton and set up an area where people can work the camera. We hung a Malibu beach scene and hired a hunky surfer to pose with the guests. The Polaroid shots were available immediately so guests could bring home some eye candy!

WHAT IS YOUR BEST PARTY TIP?

"Relax and be yourself and if you can't be yourself and be relaxed, be someone who is. Pretend you're someone fabulous, like Diane von Furstenberg; strike a pose and believe it."
— **Gigi Levangie Grazer**

"Be well rested and in good spirits, and if you bring along a date, make sure he or she is a welcome addition." — **Michael Michelle**

"Beautiful people, delicious food, great music, and lots of cocktails."
— **Alexandra von Furstenberg**

WHO WAS THERE 1. Rupert and Wendy Murdoch **2.** Elizabeth Harrison and Gretchen Mol **3.** Mitch Grazer and Kelly Lynch **4.** Brian Grazer, Ian Schrager, Donny Deutsch, and Jonathan Tisch **5.** Michael Michelle **6.** Russell Crowe and Brian Grazer **7.** Gigi Grazer and Jackie Collins **8.** Matt Minnis and Lara Shriftman **9.** Gigi Grazer and Rita Wilson

Invitations

We went for fun and frisky, just like Gigi's novel. We printed text from the book in pink on square card stock with an embossed "pink lady"—the image from the book's cover—on top of the text. The back flap of the pink envelope featured a catchy phrase from the novel: "There are starter jobs, starter cars, starter houses, and then there are starter wives." Think country-club cool, something sophisticated with an edge, and you've got the perfect invite for the classic cocktail party.

Steal It!

Instead of using traditional white or cream for the invites, rev it up with a five-by-seven-inch matte or glossy card in a vibrant color, like hot pink, lime green, or bright orange. Or print the text in a vivid color on white paper.

Pick a classic font, preferably something blockish and bold. You can use all capital letters for a strong statement.

Flush all the text to the left, creating white space along the right-hand side of the invite.

Use an image in the background of the text, like a martini or champagne glass or a wine bottle.

Get funky with the envelope as well. Create contrast with the invite by picking an envelope that matches the invitation's text color, and then print the address and return labels in white. For example, a white invite with hot-pink lettering would be enclosed in a hot-pink envelope with white lettering.

> **CHIC TIP**
> THINK OUTSIDE THE BOX WHEN IT COMES TO GIVING DIRECTIONS TO AN ENTRANCE THAT IS DIFFICULT TO FIND. AT THE BEVERLY HILTON, WE POSITIONED STAFF DRESSED IN PINK WITH VINTAGE SUITCASES IN HAND THROUGHOUT THE GROUNDS TO SERVE AS HUMAN ARROWS TO DIRECT GUESTS TO THE PARTY.

Party at Home

It's all in the details. If you're throwing a party at home, here are a few must-dos:

Clean the house from top to bottom. Check your medicine cabinet and other bathroom cabinets and hide anything you don't want the Snoopy Sally on your guest list to find.

Rearrange the furniture so people can freely mingle in some areas, and make other areas more loungelike.

Is it garbage day? If so, make sure you don't have waste bins lining your driveway, overflowing with trash. Stash that huge Hefty sack of kitchen scraps in the garage!

Check with your neighbors! Alert them to the impending traffic, parking situation, and inevitable loud music, especially if your party will go into the late hours of the night.

Serve It!

In addition to having a bar with a bartender, always hand your guests a drink the minute they walk in the door. At Harrison & Shriftman events we station servers at party entrances, with trays of both specialty cocktails and bottled water. Be sure to have plenty of water on hand. A nice touch is to have bottles of water right by the door so partygoers can hydrate on their way home.

> "PLACE VINEGAR IN SMALL CUPS ALL AROUND YOUR HOUSE AFTER THE PARTY TO HELP SUCK ALL THE SMOKY SMELLS OUT OF YOUR FURNITURE, CURTAINS, ETC."
> —Molly Sims

Gift Bags

We created a *Starter Wife* kit filled with all the Hollywood essentials, including gift certificates for BOTOX, for service at Mobile Tanning Pros, and for an aura reading. Plus, we indulged the shopping instincts of every woman and set up an exclusive UGG store featuring a shoe display and a seating area for trying shoes on. The female guests could select baby-blue or pale-pink UGG boots and purses, while the men were gifted with chestnut-colored boots. And, of course, each guest left with a signed copy of *The Starter Wife*.

Steal It!

Get inspired by the theme of the party and create a unique parting gift. For a classic cocktail party, just about anything goes. But here are some of our favorite goody-bag fillers:

The recipe for a specialty drink poured the evening of the party, along with the necessary mixers

Candles, photo frames, and a tin of mints

A mixed CD of cocktail tunes. You can hand out the one you created for the party or have one specially made

A bottle of top-shelf liquor, slipped in a simple velvet bag

A box of delicious chocolate truffles

Drinks

A full bar is no longer a necessity, even at a cocktail party. You can serve red and white wine along with one signature cocktail or create a few whimsical beverages inspired by the party's theme. Always be sure to offer a nonalcoholic selection.

The Pink Lady
(a classic pink-lemonade martini)

The Divorce

Malibu Splash

For the Love of Vanilla Crème

Voss water

The Menu

When throwing a classic cocktail party, you want the food to match the mood. In Los Angeles, we adapted the Polo Lounge dinner menu and made the items miniature. Guests want to drink and mingle and stave off hunger with a few tasty tidbits. At any party where cocktails are the focus, never serve anything that requires juggling a dinner plate and silverware!

In New York, we served delicious sushi from Nobu. Not only was this a huge draw for guests, as the restaurant is one of Manhattan's best, but it also was a tie-in to scenes from the novel.

McCarthy salad atop wonton cups

Bloody Mary oyster shooter

Gazpacho shooter in cucumber cups

Dungeness-crab cakes with grain-mustard sauce

Mini-hamburgers

Smoked chicken with cilantro, mango, and papaya salsa

Lobster corn dogs

Sweet-potato frites

Mini pink-and-white chocolate-coconut cupcakes, with the pink lady image on top of the cupcake

Serve It!

As we've stated (but we can't stress it enough!), passing both hors d'ouevres and desserts around on trays is definitely the best method for serving them. Another fun presentation is serving the food in edible dishes; for example, our gazpacho shooters were served in a cucumber cup. It's easier to eat this way, and guests aren't left holding a skewer or an empty container. If your party has a theme, bring the details full circle by including your servers; our waitstaff wore *Starter Wife* T-shirts. Black pants and pressed white shirts are also ideal for any cocktail party.

Everyone *pretends* they don't eat dessert, but they really do! Always serve something sweet so guests can indulge a little. You can keep it simple with an assortment of cookies alongside a healthy snack of fruit, like strawberries and raspberries, or go all out and set up a dessert bar with all the decadent doings: brownies, cupcakes, biscotti, tarts, and more.

CHIC TIP
WHEN PLANNING A COCKTAIL-PARTY MENU, STRIVE TO HAVE A MINIMUM OF THREE COLD AND THREE HOT APPETIZERS.

Cookies by Design cookies printed with *The Starter Wife* book cover on them (perfect for any party because you can scan any design onto the cookie).

It's a Pleasure Doing Business

A Product Launch Party

The Day-Glo concert hall at Paris's fragrance launch.

At a product launch party, making a lasting impression is all about creating an event that reflects a brand's style. Before you decide on a plan of action, ask the company that makes the product how they want it marketed: Fun and frisky? Elegant and classy? We've thrown classic cocktail parties, color-themed events, and even a pool party for the various products we have launched, which include Juicy Couture's swim and yoga apparel, Jimmy Choo (USA) shoes, and Christian Dior watches. At this party Parlux Fragrances, the company behind Paris Hilton's signature scent, sponsored the soiree, so the evening melded Paris's business and social worlds. It's all about making the event work for the brand!

News flash: Business events can be unusual, creative, and, most important, fun. A successful launch party reflects the product and the host, and both should make a lasting impression on every guest. When it came time to plan a fête for Paris Hilton's perfume by Parlux Fragrances, we knew it had to be as fabulous as she is. So we threw a glamorous late-night dance party and invited more than five hundred guests to celebrate from 9:00 p.m. to the wee hours of the morning.

We took over two floors of an empty office building and transformed them into three distinct areas, each one offering a different vibe: conversational chic, boogie central, and head-banging loud. Downstairs it was a paradise of white drapes and loungy vignettes, with a disco dance floor off to the side. Upstairs we created an all-black rocker's haven with fluorescent graffiti–covered walls, which also set the stage for a punk performance by Juliette Lewis's band, Juliette and the Licks.

We incorporated the perfume, Paris Hilton by Paris Hilton, and the product's signature black-and-pink packaging, throughout the décor. For example, we hung full-length posters from the ad campaign on the elevator doors so that when the doors opened, Paris appeared to be welcoming guests. Since the launch was bicoastal, we re-created the Los Angeles bash in New York, where we featured a similar sultry pink lounge.

Whether you plan to introduce the next big thing or simply want to turn your basement into a hot club for New Year's Eve, this chapter will give you a slew of stellar ideas. What're ya waiting for? It's party time!

Even if you're not launching a product of any sort, this party is a great template for learning how to transform a raw space like a garage or a bare-bones conference room. In our case, we turned an empty two-story office building into an amazing pink palace that suited Paris's true princess style. The venue was split into two separate floors, with cement flooring and unfinished walls. Sound daunting? Think again! This was a best-case scenario, as we had a completely blank canvas and could do whatever our hearts desired. Take another look—doesn't that garage have tons of promise? Thought so!

> "IF YOU WANT PEOPLE TO SOCIALIZE, EITHER KEEP THE MUSIC TO WHERE GUESTS DON'T HAVE TO SHOUT OR DEDICATE AN AREA FOR DANCING WHERE THE MUSIC DOESN'T DISTURB OTHERS."
> —REGINA KING

Juliette and the
Licks performed.

Location

Throwing a party at a night-club can make planning easier since you don't have to worry about décor: the seating, flowers, and lighting are already in place. But it can get costly.

You'll want to get down to nitty gritty decisions like whether you are springing for an open bar all night long or attaching a price limit so that when that amount is reached the party changes to a cash bar. Other options include bottle service at tables or serving a specialty drink gratis while the rest is cash. Also be sure to find out who will be offering the DJ services: Do you need to provide your own or will the club take care of the music? Make a list of all of your requirements so that when you meet with the manager of each club you can quickly decide which establishment meets your needs.

CHIC TIP

WHEN WORKING WITH SPACE THAT IS TOO BIG, USE CURTAIN SHEERS TO CREATE A SMALLER, MORE WORKABLE SETTING. CREATE COZY VIGNETTE SEATING BY HANGING SHEERS TO BLOCK OFF DIFFERENT AREAS THROUGH-OUT THE ROOM. THE FILMY FABRIC ALLOWS GUESTS TO SEE THE ENTIRE SPACE AT THE SAME TIME THAT IT CREATES A MORE INTIMATE SPACE FOR GATHERING.

The New York
party décor—
loungy and sexy.

The downstairs featured soft, romantic lighting from candles and Kartell lamps, while upstairs the club was dimly lit, with bright strobe-light flashes to set the concert mood.

Steal It!

Place white votive candles in clear votive holders wrapped in various shades of pink cellophane paper.

Cover spotlights with pink gels and position them to create sultry uplighting.

How to Wrap Votive-Candle Holders

1. Buy adhesive cellophane and votive-candle holders.

2. Measure the circumference of the votive holder and cut the cellophane to fit.

3. Remove the adhesive backing from the cellophane and wrap the cellophane around the votive holder. Be sure to press the cellophane evenly to avoid creases and wrinkles.

4. Drop the votive candle inside the holder and light it.

The Playlist

At our party there was something for everyone, whether guests were in the mood to bang their heads, dance to Beyoncé, or just chill out. The concert hall featured the rockin' Juliette Lewis and her band, Juliette and the Licks, while the downstairs lounge featured chill ambient tunes. In the dance hall, next to the lounge, a DJ spun a cool mix of dance tunes. Paris even got in the mood and surprised the guests by singing a few tunes from her upcoming album. For any kind of nightclub party, you want to play the latest, hottest songs to get people in the party mood.

Décor

For the Los Angeles event, we completely transformed an empty office building into Paris's pink palace. Downstairs, a large open room became a sultry lounge featuring fluffy white couches and hot-pink sofas, with generous splashes of pink everywhere, from the pillows and fabrics to the candles and lamps. To further camouflage the bare office surroundings, full-length photos of Paris Hilton covered the elevator doors. Since the space was so huge, we hung pink sheers to hide the office walls and to create cozy seating areas. To the right of the lounge, we created a dance floor with a huge disco ball and strobe lights.

Upstairs, the venue featured an all-black concert hall with fluorescent and neon accents. To give it a cool underground vibe, the walls were spray painted with graffiti designs and messages. A wall-sized chalkboard was hung on the back wall, allowing guests to pen personalized messages to Paris.

The New York party followed the same color scheme and had the same sultry vibe, with big, cushy daybeds, couches, and ottomans and soft, rosy lighting.

Steal It!

Create a space for lounging by tightly grouping daybeds and ottomans next to side tables adorned with flowers.

Use a white palette to make the signature color pop. For example, at our party the white daybeds were piled up with pillows in various shades of pink.

Create a glam mood with crystal chandeliers and Kartell lamps.

Place various sizes of pillar candles on square mirrors.

Party Highlight: The party was three events packed into one, and each setting offered a different vibe. Whatever mood guests were in, there was a place for them to party.

WHAT IS YOUR BEST PARTY ADVICE?

"Always roll with a bunch of your closest girlfriends."
— **Nicky Hilton**

"Advance planning!"
— **Paulina Rubio**

"Have good decorations and lighting. Set the mood."
— **Kristin Cavallari**

"If it's your party, don't drink too much; if it is someone else's, have fun no matter what. I think fun is a choice that everyone makes, so make it and you'll see how easy it is to have it." — **Bijou Phillips**

"Never be the first to arrive, and when you do arrive, make a great entrance." — **Sarah Michelle Gellar**

BILLY BOB THORNTON'S MUSIC TIP: "PLAY NO DOUBT!"

WHO WAS THERE 1. Paris Hilton with the event staff **2.** Rick and Kathy Hilton **3.** Paris Hilton and Elisa Cuthbert **4.** Kevin Connolly and Adrian Grenier **5.** Oksana Baiul **6.** Paris Hilton and Elizabeth Harrison **7.** Paris Hilton, Chad Muska, and Kyle Richards **8.** Paris and Nicky Hilton

Invitations

It is imperative that the invite mirror the product being showcased. We captured Paris Hilton's princess style by sending tiaras tucked in a black velour pouch that was tied with a pink ribbon and attached to the invitation. Make sure the invite gives your guests an instant sense of what kind of event they are attending—and, most important, why.

Steal It!

1. Purchase tiaras and black velour or velvet pouches from a wholesale vendor.

2. Put the invites on pink card stock using labels (we recommend Avery 8163).

3. Print the labels and cut them using a paper cutter.

4. Using a hole puncher, punch a hole through each pink label and tie it to the black pouch with a pink ribbon.

Be creative! Other cute ideas could include using a compact, a perfume bottle, an empty perfume box with the invite rolled inside, or a perfume label on a flat piece of paper with the party details printed in the center.

The invite should reflect the mood and style of the product so that guests automatically associate the invite with the product. Harrison & Shriftman is known for creating memorable invites, like Paris's tiara and the Juicy Couture kickboards. A few tips to keep in mind:

Incorporate the font, colors, and style of the product or use the actual product and attach the invitation with a ribbon. You could also glue it onto the product box.

Make sure the invite stands out so guests notice it among their bills and magazines: Make it oversized, use colored envelopes, or include a prop like the tiara.

Flowers

At the LA party a huge flower wall was constructed at the end of the pink "red carpet" to separate the outdoor smoking patio from the party entrance. Inside, roses in assorted shades of pink were wrapped in faux-leather corsets, and small roses were placed in white ornamental boxes on side tables. In New York, floral vases replicated the black-and-white design of the perfume bottle.

How to Make Ottomans

You will need:

Standard plastic milk crates from a grocery store. Use one or ten, depending on your seating needs.

Two-inch foam, enough to cover all four sides of the crate and the top.

Fabric in a catchy color or print that matches your décor. Be sure to measure your crate and then add a few additional feet of fabric to allow for mistakes.

A hot glue gun.

A staple gun.

Scissors.

1. Cut four pieces of two-inch foam to the same size as the sides of the milk crate. The foam for the top of the crate should be cut with an extra two inches on all four sides so it will cover the other foam pieces.

2. Apply a layer of hot glue to the edges of the foam and attach all five pieces to the milk crate.

3. Remeasure the size of the crate: the length, width, and height. Cut the fabric to the appropriate size. Be sure to add a few extra inches so you can staple the material to the inside opening of the crate.

4. Position the crate in the middle of the fabric, pull the fabric tight, and begin stapling the fabric to the sides inside the open edge of the crate. You will need to make some extra folds in the fabric in order to get nice tight edges so that there are no wrinkles in the fabric.

5. Flip the crate over, and *voilà!* A cozy extra seat.

Gift Bags

Upon exiting the party, our guests received an "I Love Paris" T-shirt, Paris Hilton perfume, and CDs by Juliette and the Licks. In addition, since it was an unusually cold night, we featured a coffee stand outside at the valet area so guests could warm up with a cappuccino or an espresso. The valets also handed each guest a pink rose.

Steal It!

Create a gift bag centered on the featured product. If the product is too expensive, then give something else from the same brand, like a gift certificate.

CHIC TIP
IF YOU CAN'T GIVE OUT A FABULOUS GIFT, THEN DON'T GIVE OUT ANYTHING AT ALL! DON'T FILL A BAG WITH A BUNCH OF CHEAP JUNK, ESPECIALLY AT A PRODUCT LAUNCH PARTY.

Menu

Since it was a late-night party, we created a menu of finger foods that were "sleepover chic." Everyone loves to eat diner-type food, so we took that craving and made it upscale! And don't forget, everyone loves to nibble on desserts, just keep them mini.

HORS D'OEUVRES
Provide tray service for the hors d'oeuvres.

Mini round pizzas

Mac 'n' cheese croquettes

Pigs in a blanket, with honey-dijon dipping sauce, tomatillo salsa, and guacamole

Bite-sized grilled Beverly Hills sirloin burgers and cheeseburgers, with caramelized-onion marmalade and homemade ketchup

Mini Monte Cristo sandwiches

Chicken barbecue turnovers

Crab cakes

DESSERTS
Provide tray service for the desserts.

Petit fours with Eiffel Towers iced on top

Mini marshmallow cupcakes

Serve It!

Cute blond servers dressed in "I Love Paris" tees and wearing tiaras provided tray service for all the hors d'oeuvres and desserts. Note that how food is styled is just as important as its taste; for example, we served Monte Cristo sandwiches cut into tiny triangles and stacked neatly on serving trays.

Cover the bottom of serving trays with stones from a floral shop or with the buds of pink flowers.

Line up cupcakes in a neat row on black Mikasa trays.

Cut sandwiches into triangles or use a cookie cutter to create cool shapes and designs.

Serve all dipping sauces in clear bowls along with the hors d'oeuvres.

CHIC TIP
NOT A BETTY CROCKER BAKER? DON'T STRESS OUT OVER MEASURING FLOUR AND COCOA POWDER; HEAD TO THE GROCERY STORE AND FILL UP YOUR SHOPPING CART WITH HOSTESS CUPCAKES, BROWNIE MIXES, AND TONS OF CANDY. BE PLAYFUL WHEN YOU ARRANGE THE DESSERTS ON TRAYS AND PLATTERS—ADD SOME COLOR AND A FEW TEXTURED ELEMENTS LIKE MARBLES OR FLOWER PETALS.

Drinks

One large circular bar was featured in the middle of all the action downstairs, while upstairs the bar was located next to the stage. To match the pink-palace setting, we served rosy-colored beverages and even created a signature cocktail in honor of Paris. Drinks were also available from the servers that circulated throughout the room with trays.

Cranberry champagne

Cosmolitos

Cans of pink Mixed Berry 7-Up Plus, served with bright pink straws

Sofia Blanc de Blancs sparkling wine cans

Slumber-party chic:
Everyone loves
Hostess cupcakes.

At a party for
*Team America:
World Police.*

theme parties

We love coming up with new and festive concepts, such as the sugar-spun birthday party, and taking our guests on ethnic tours like the Asian-inspired fête we threw for the *Team America: World Police* premiere. Best of all, you don't need a special date to throw a theme party; coming up with a cool concept is reason enough! Once you've settled on your fabulous bash, set the pace from the beginning. Pick an invitation that conveys the personality of your party and be sure to let guests know what to expect: Do they need to dress up like their favorite rock star (bring on the Mick Jaggers!) or wear a certain color?

Another key to the theme party is crafting the ambience. Don't hold back when it comes to decorating; drench the décor in theme elements. Express the idea in every manner possible—think about the lighting, the flowers, the menu, and so on. If you're planning a color-infused event like our yellow Tweety launch party go for lighting and floral arrangements in your theme color. In honor of a breakup, you could throw a blues party—think crawfish étouffée and jambalaya, BB King tunes, and blue couches and throw pillows. Whatever concept puts you in the mood to party will also have your guests raring to go.

We've put together some of our favorite themes—they're sure to make a fabulous night—but anything goes with theme parties. Just pick something you love, whether it's sports, cooking, or glam rock music, and go crazy!

Starry, Starry Night: Make the evening mystical by throwing an astrological party with every kind of soothsayer available. Set up stations for a palm reader, tea leaf reader, tarot card reader, numerologist, and even a fortune teller complete with a crystal ball! Don't forget to break out the Ouija board.

Come On, Barbie, Let's Go Party! Have your guests dress up as their favorite Barbie or Ken.

Naughty 'n' Nice: Have a leather-and-lace party, or dress as secretary hos and CEOs.

***Dynasty* Darling:** Gaudy over-the-top glamour is the goal of this party. Have all your guests come dressed as their favorite *Dynasty* character, with big hair, lots of makeup, costume jewelry, and furs. Pop in a DVD of your favorite season and let the catfights begin! Of course, this idea is great for any soapy show, including *Dallas; Melrose Place; Beverly Hills, 90210; The OC; and Desperate Housewives.*

Get Lucky: Bring Las Vegas to your home by creating a minicasino. Set up tables for poker, blackjack, and craps and hand out fake money.

Pretty in Pink: Invite all your best gal pals over for a *Legally Blonde* night in which everything is dripping in pink. Keep it totally girlie by having manicures, pedicures, and facials.

Denim and Diamonds: Rent space at a stable, barn, or any place with a Western feel or decorate your backyard with hay bales and old wagon wheels. Break out the cowboy boots and chaps, and enjoy the rowdy ride. Don't forget to rent a mechanical bull.

Era Party: Turn the night into a time capsule by picking your favorite decade (twenties, thirties, forties, seventies) and step into the past. Design the space with elements from the selected time period, so if it's '70s go for tie-dyed material and lava lamps.

'80s Prom: Party like it's 1989 by spraying your hair with Aqua Net. Hand out corsages and make sure the guys and girls put on their best prom outfits. Set up a space where guests can take their prom-night picture.

Retro Game Bash: Gather up the gang for rounds of Dominos, Twister, Connect Four, Monopoly, and a little spin-the-bottle action.

Roller Ball: Get ready to boogie. Rent out a roller-skating rink and have everyone dress up in their best Studio 54 wear.

partying for a good cause

HOW TO TURN ANY EVENT INTO A FUND-RAISER

Charity benefits are a key aspect of every community. You can take any party and turn it into a fund-raiser—it's as easy as it sounds. A shopping party, theme dinner, or black-tie gala can become a fund-raiser when you simply donate the proceeds *(ch-ching!)* from ticket sales, clothing purchases, or an auction to a charity that means something to you. The options as to how you can raise the money are endless, and since people naturally love parties, a charitable element makes the event even more alluring. Best of all, when people come to a charity function, they arrive in the mood to spend money, and leave with a good feeling.

We've done so many wonderful benefits, including the Love Heals party to raise money for AIDS education and Motorola's parties benefiting Toys for Tots. We've gathered the best and easiest ways to raise a ton of moolah while giving your guests an evening to remember.

The Classic Fund-Raiser: This is where people pay to attend the event. Send out an invitation card in advance, with the ticket cost or suggested contribution. To accommodate last-minute impulses, allow guests to pay at the door the night of the party.

Pay the Price: Ticket amounts can be broken down a variety of ways, usually either by person or table. In both cases location determines the price, with prime spaces next to the stage (when the event includes a performance), close to the bar, or near the dance floor; these prime spaces will be more expensive than other spots. A lot of huge New York fund-raisers have "junior" tickets: Instead of buying a table or a seat at a table, you can buy an after-dinner ticket, which is a less expensive option. If the event is at a bar, you can charge a cover fee and have all the money go to charity.

Late-Night Club Party: A fund-raiser doesn't have to be a seated dinner; a new thing we love to do at Harrison & Shriftman is to offer lounge and vignette seating. In addition to giving a donation to attend the party, guests can increase the amount contributed by reserving a VIP lounge or area so they can chill with their friends.

All-Day Shopping Extravaganza: This is a fantastic way to raise money. Have boutiques and fashion designers set up shopping booths at a local gym, fairground, or theater, or anywhere with a large open space. Shoppers can make a small donation at the entrance, and a portion of the proceeds can go to charity. Every year in the Hamptons, we work on Super Saturday, an event for ovarian cancer research, where designers and boutique owners congregate to sell their goods for charity.

Shop Till Ya Drop: A boutique party like our yellow-themed Tweety party is a perfect fund-raising opportunity; simply have a percentage of the sales go to a specified charity. Many boutiques already set aside days when they donate a portion of sales to charity. Approach boutique owners in your town and see what you can get started.

Host with the Most: For large-scale charity functions, always have a host committee. These people will work to get everything done, including selling tickets and obtaining donations. Every single person has a different set of social and business contacts, which can be instrumental in putting together an event—so the more people involved, the better.

Bidding Wars: Live and silent auctions are phenomenal ways to raise money and can be an element at any party. At a silent auction, get the fund-raising started by setting up an area with all the goods displayed so guests can freely browse. Be sure to include bid sheets listing the opening price and total prize value—and watch the dollars roll in! The key to a live auction is an emcee with an amazing personality. For example, at the annual Butterfly

Ball benefiting Chrysalis, director Brett Ratner helped raise more than a hundred thousand dollars!

Bring a Gift: During the holidays add a charity element to your party by having guests bring a wrapped present. At a Just Cavalli's holiday bash, we asked each guest to bring a toy for Para Los Niños. At the end of the night, we had amassed thousands of goodies!

Corporate Contributions: Research companies that donate money, especially those that support your cause. Write a proper business letter (usually to the public-relations office) thoroughly explaining the event: the date, the time, the place, how many people will attend, and what you would like from their company. For example, you may ask a company to sponsor your event, donate items for the gift bag, or help with the auction. Let them know how you will acknowledge their contribution, be it on the invite, in the program, or by prominently displaying their goods. Companies love to get involved, because it gets their goods into the hands of consumers. We did an event sponsored by Revlon and created centerpieces filled with makeup at all the tables so guests could try their products.

Get the Goods: Ask companies, designers, boutiques, spas, restaurants, and travel organizations to donate items like a hotel stay, dinner for four, airline tickets, a spa certificate, clothing items, and so on. Guests love it, but, best of all, everyone benefits from auctions: The charity receives money, the companies get great exposure, and the guests get fabulous treats, like a trip to Tahiti at a much lower cost than they otherwise would have paid.

Know the Rules: Many charity organizations have guidelines, so be sure you have a clear understanding of their business practices.

WHAT IS THE BEST PARTY YOU HAVE EVER BEEN TO, AND WHY?

"I loved Ed Limato's Academy Awards party every year—lots of interesting people, great food, and great music, and Ed is a fabulous host. Also, love the Vanity Fair party. Everyone always ends up there at some point. One of the most fun parties I've ever been to was one that I gave with Allan Carr and Stan Dragoti. I was getting divorced and moving out of the house I had lived in with Rod. We decided to give one final big blast for New Year's Eve. It was in the ballroom, and we had a band play first, then a trio called the Step Sisters, who sang all '40s songs and then went into the '50s and '60s. At midnight, forty bagpipers appeared, to bring in the New Year. People still tell me it was one the best parties they have ever been to."   — **Alana Stewart**

"Diddy's party in New York for fashion week. Everybody was there. He had the best music— I loved it."   — **Paulina Rubio**

"Lara's pimps-and-hos party. Costume parties are the best!"   — **Nicky Hilton**

"Bianca Jagger's birthday party at Studio 54."
    — **Michael Kors**

"There was a maverick party at Spy Bar in New York, maybe it was '96—it was insane. I always count that as the all-time best party I've been to. I'm sure being sixteen had something to do with it; everything is great at that age."   — **Bijou Phillips**

"John Travolta's 50th B-day. It was in Cabo San Lucas and lasted all weekend. It was like an unreal episode of *This Is Your Life*. Roberta Flack and Carly Simon performed, as well as just about every other legend. No detail was overlooked: personal concierge services as well as Alka-Seltzer on your pillow. The vibe was great—so much love for one person."   — **Forest Whitaker**

"Every birthday party for my kids."
    — **Billy Bob Thornton**

"The next one..."   — **Lara Flynn Boyle**

toasts of the town

Giving the perfect toast turns an ordinary occasion into an extraordinary celebration. But before you grab your pen and start crafting a twenty-minute speech, heed our advice and make it short, sweet, and snappy. Nothing ruins a party faster than a terrible toast—don't try and be the funny guy or write up a three-page acceptance-letter-cum-speech.

Make a fabulous statement by using a tried-and-true toast, a famous quote or poem, or even a line from a movie that sums up the moment. If you need to say something incredibly special, a great starting point is finding a line or proverb that almost fits and making it your own by adding a memory or a personal thought. But whatever you say, just get to the point, quickly! And remember, when you end the toast, raise your glass and look everyone in the eye. *Clink, clink!*

TOAST TIPS

"I only thank everyone for coming to make it a special evening."
– **Dani Janssen**

"The best toasts are always from the heart. Speak your mind. Lie, in a pinch." – **David Arquette**

"Unrehearsed and from the heart. And short." – **Peter Som**

"One from the heart and spirit...I say what I feel for the person."
– **Forest Whitaker**

Here are a few of our favorites

"Here's looking at you, kid."
—Humphrey Bogart
in *Casablanca*

"Carpe diem, seize the day, boys, make your lives extraordinary."
—*Dead Poets Society*

"When choosing between two evils, I always like to take the one I never tried before." —Mae West

"For better or worse, but never for granted." —Arlene Dahl

"Three be the things I shall never attain, / Envy, content and sufficient champagne." —Dorothy Parker

"The best and most beautiful things in the world cannot be seen, nor even touched, but just felt in the heart." —Helen Keller

"Love doesn't make the world go round, but it sure makes the ride worthwhile." —Franklin P. Jones

"Here's to lying, cheating, and stealing. Lie to save a friend, cheat to cheat death, steal to steal the heart of someone you love."
—Irish Blessing

"May you live as long as you want, and may you never want as long as you live." —Irish Blessing

CELEBRITY TOASTS

"I love you, and you are truly someone I can say is a real friend."
– **Michael Michelle**

"May the best day of your past be the worst day of your future."
– **Sarah Michelle Gellar**

"Dans les yeux!" ("In the eyes!")
– **Molly Sims**

"If you slide down the banister of life, I hope the splinters are kind."
– **Lara Flynn Boyle**

"Bottoms up—there's more where this came from." – **Billy Bob Thornton**

"Here's to love, money, and health."
– **Michael Kors**

"To life, love, and happiness. *Salud!*"
– **Rita Schrager**

"Wishing everyone many blessings from God and good health and double happiness." – **Venus Williams**

Great Toast Books

Crisp Toasts: Wonderful Words That Add Wit and Class to Every Time You Raise Your Glass by Andrew Frothingham and William R. Evans

Toasts for Every Occasion by Jennifer Rahel Conover

Toasts: Over 1,500 of the Best Toasts, Sentiments, Blessings, and Graces by Paul Dickson

the ultimate Hollywood hostess: Dani Janssen

The legendary Hollywood doyenne Dani Janssen is famous for her triple-A-list and super-exclusive Oscar soirees thrown at her apartment. Her annual ultra-private dinner is Hollywood's most sought-after party of the year. She extends invitations to an eclectic but very select group of about 100 people that includes Jack Nicholson, Clint Eastwood, Harrison Ford, Steven Spielberg, Tom Hanks, Oprah Winfrey, Bruce and Patti Springsteen, and Quincy Jones.

Her effervescent personality makes her a phenomenal hostess but even more so, Dani plans and executes the perfect party, every time. She handles every single detail herself from making decorations for the table to cooking the dinner. Dani is especially famous for her "monkey bread." And at the end of the night she hands out the ultimate gift bag: She heads to the freezer and pulls out preprepared dishes of everyone's favorite meal and sends guests home with a lovingly packaged dinner in a brown paper bag.

Dani's Top Party Tips
• "Organize and plan every detail before the party. Make notes and lists (including notes on your wardrobe) for every single day of the week before the party.
• "On the last day, write a list for all the help, even the kitchen staff. Write down how to manage everything from the kitchen to placing the china to putting serving pots in the correct cupboard once they are cleaned.
• "Put the list on the wall in the kitchen so everyone can refer to it."

Best Party Advice
• "No cameras. Only use your personal one. Take pictures all night and send them out approximately one year later with the invitation to the following year's party. It will remind the guests of how much fun they had at your last party."

WHAT IS THE BEST PARTY YOU'VE EVER BEEN TO, AND WHY?

"My last wedding...there were seven hundred people dressed in Western wear; otherwise they weren't allowed in. It was held on the Western street of Universal Studios' back lot, where a bunting read, "There's going to be a hitching here tonight." The wedding was so large Universal gave it a production number.

"I wanted it to be an authentic 1800s wedding. Three days before, Hal's caterer, with earth diggers, dug out a pit large enough to fill with mesquite wood and coals. Over this was a tin piece, and on top were sides of beef and pork, turkey, and chicken. The studio hired firemen to watch the pit.

"The wedding cake, a three-layered spice cake from an 1800s recipe, decorated with frosting and baby's breath, was six by ten feet—so large, it had to be placed on a buckboard wagon. I rode up to the church in a black carriage covered with gardenias (my favorite flower) and pulled by a team of matching black horses, with a driver in top hat and tails. My lace dress was also from the 1800s.

"I walked up the stairs to the outside altar to marry Hal Needham. Burt Reynolds was the best man. Burt and Hal rode up on matching black (stunt) horses with sterling-silver-mounted saddles. When they arrived at the church, Hal quietly said, 'Down,' and his horse knelt to the ground as Hal stepped off. The guests went wild.

"After the nuptials, the scent of the open mesquite pit hit the air. The line was a hundred feet long. There were beans in a black pot that was big enough to bathe in. Bartenders used Mason jars that they threw in the air behind them, caught, and filled with drinks, which they then slid down the bar to stop in front of whoever had ordered them.

"Tanya Tucker and Glen Campbell sang to Mel Tillis's band, and guests were taught how to line dance on a dance floor surrounded by hay bales."

best host gifts

With all the parties we throw and attend, we're accustomed to both giving and receiving gifts. Thinking of something new and creative can be hard, especially when it comes to those who have everything—or are always receiving presents. The key to a wonderful host gift is to give something the person wants or needs. But don't stress out searching for the perfect gift; it can be something as simple as a scented candle, a great bottle of wine, such as an '82 Lafite, or top-shelf vodka. The present doesn't have to be big and expensive as long as it's thoughtful, like a stack of photos cinched with a bow and sealed in a pretty white box.

While we all adore flowers, don't arrive at the party with a bunch in hand. The host has to drop everything, dig out a vase, and arrange the blossoms to match the décor. Instead, send flowers either before or after the party, with a handwritten note thanking them for their hospitality (communicate the note to the florist beforehand so it's personal). Make blossoms even more special by finding out the host's favorite flower or florist; for example, orchids are Lara Shriftman's favorite, and she adores any arrangement by florist Eric Buterbaugh.

Finally, make a beautiful presentation. You can have the gift professionally wrapped or can do it yourself by decorating the envelope or box and tying it with tons of pretty ribbons. And always, *always* include a handwritten personal note on a nice piece of stationery or card.

Since we simply adore giving—and receiving—gifts, we've put together some of our favorite host gifts that are perfect for any occasion.

BOOKS

A First-Edition Book: This is an excellent choice for someone who has everything, since it is special and very unique. It can be an art, a photography, or a fashion book, a complete set of Nancy Drew novels, or anything that especially interests the host.

Coffee Table Books: People love coffee table books, so look for something from museums, such as John Lautner architecture books or art books. We love Ed Ruscha; *The Secret Language of Birthdays;* or just a great selection of biographies and fashion, photography, and Old Hollywood titles.

A Full Set of Entertaining Books: Every host needs a collection of entertaining books, and we just love Ina Garten's. She's a great hostess with wonderful tips.

A Full Set of Restaurant Cookbooks: As with the entertaining collection, every host needs a great set of cookbooks. These will inspire their menu selections. Again, don't give just one; create a wonderful group that includes the host's favorite restaurants and chefs. Some of our favorites are *Nobu: The Cookbook, Eat at Joe's: The Joe's Stone Crab Restaurant Cookbook, The Harry's Bar Cookbook, The Palm Restaurant Cookbook,* and *The Magnolia Bakery Cookbook: Old-Fashioned Recipes from New York's Sweetest Bakery.*

Jackie Collins Novels: Who doesn't love *Lucky* or *Hollywood Divorces?* Every girl needs to indulge in fun, sexy beach reading, and Jackie Collins romance novels are perfect. Don't give just one—give the entire set.

Ronnie Gousman Photo Albums and Scrapbooks: This is Hollywood's best-kept secret: Every Hollywood director gets their scripts and clippings bound by Gousman. Each one is customized, so you can pick the color of the leather and the look of the pages. You can even personalize the look and text on the cover. A gift like this is perfect because everyone needs more places to store pictures and hold special things.

GIFT CERTIFICATES

Calligraphy: For someone who plans a ton of parties, giving a new resource is always appreciated. Stephannie Barba and Bernard Maisner are two of our favorites.

A Visit to a Salon: Send a gift certificate for hair and makeup or for a visit to a day spa at a place like Frederic Fekkai, Oribe, John Barrett, the Four Seasons, Cornelia day spa, or any place equally fabulous in your hometown. Just be sure to send the certificate beforehand so the host can indulge prior to the big event.

Private Training: If your host loves working out, then give them a private training session at the gym. Other ideas include a gift certificate for a yoga, spinning, or kickboxing class.

Record Store: If your host is less technically inclined or into deejaying, give them a great set of CDs. If you're not sure of their taste, opt for a gift certificate from a record store so they can choose their own CDs or vinyl records.

Bucks for Books: If your host already has an extensive library, help them add to their collection with a gift card for a local bookstore or a national chain like Amazon.com or Barnes & Noble. This way they can splurge on any set of books they desire.

Cater to Their Whims: Again, for someone who throws lots of parties, a gift certificate for catering is a thoughtful gesture. Not only does it introduce them to a new resource, but it also allows them to splurge on flowers or invites at their next get-together.

Movie Night: A great gift for a movie buff is a set of DVDs. Send the host a bunch of romance films, like *When Harry Met Sally...*, *Sleepless in Seattle,* and *An Affair to Remember,* or a group of Harrison Ford flicks. Add a bag of microwave popcorn and it's the perfect movie night. Don't know their taste? Give a gift certificate to Netflix so they can choose their own!

FOOD AND DRINKS

Mix it up! Help stock the host's bar by giving him a set of mixers, a cocktail shaker, bar utensils, or a tray. And everyone needs an incredible bottle of wine, vodka, or scotch.

Water, Water, Everywhere! Everyone drinks bottled water, so treat your host to water delivery for a month.

Serendipity 3 Frrrozen Hot Chocolate

Mrs. Beasley's Miss Grace lemon cakes

Eli's Essentials: This company offers gift baskets, like the breakfast basket, which is filled with croissants, jams, berry granola, oatmeal, coffee, and tea.

A Basket of Sauces: Simply gather a bunch of bottled sauces sold at restaurants like Nobu, Giorgio Baldi, Raos, Peter Luger, and Jean-Georges Vongerichten, and group them neatly in a basket.

WE ALSO ADORE

Personalized Stationery and Thank-You Cards: A beautiful set of cards or stationery from Cartier, Tiffany & Co., or Mrs. John L. Strong Fine Stationery.

Picture Frames: Everyone needs more picture frames, and we especially love those from Ralph Lauren and Calvin Klein. Make it extra special by taking a picture at the party, developing it the next day, and dropping it off or sending it by messenger to the host as a keepsake of all the fun you had the previous night.

Digital Camera and Printer: At Harrison & Shriftman parties, we love setting up an area where guests can get their photo taken and then print the picture so that they can take it home with them at the end of the night.

Customized iPod: If you know your host's musical taste, an amazing gift is a preprogrammed iPod with tons of great music.

Nat Sherman Colored Cigarettes: This high-end tobacco company is an indulgence for those who smoke.

Robes and Slippers: The host can slip out of her dress and shoes and dive into a cozy bathrobe—the perfect way to unwind after a great night!

Candles, Candles, and More Candles: Need we say more? When in doubt you can never go wrong with candles. Or go chic and give the new trend in incense, aroma sticks, which have amazing scents like gardenia, lavender, and more.

Dinner Goodies: Every host always needs great new serving bowls, platters, name-card holders, vases, funky silverware, barware, candlesticks, and, of course, acrylic servingware for events held outside.

Glassware: We love crystal glasses from Hermès, Baccarat, and Saint-Louis. You can buy two and continue to add to the set.

Monthly Floral Delivery: Why send one arrangement when you can send more?

Lottery Tickets: A fun and inexpensive gift that could be worth millions!

Games: These make light-hearted and fun gifts that ensure another get-together. Send the host games like Monopoly, Twister, and Cranium.

A Magazine Subscription

WHAT IS THE BEST HOST GIFT YOU EVER RECEIVED?

"Given the morning after: hair of the dog."
—**Lara Flynn Boyle**

"My friend Dwight gave me a skeleton in a baseball uniform for the Fourth of July." —**Billy Bob Thornton**

"I always love getting food." —**Peter Som**

"Caviar, always!" —**Michael Kors**

"A surprise guest." —**Allison Sarofim**

"My wife loves monogrammed stuff...once someone gave us a monogrammed martini shaker with all the fixings...that was cool." —**Forest Whitaker**

budget and seal the deal:

NEGOTIATING THE CONTRACT

Once you've settled on a venue, the next step is negotiating a contract. Whether you're renting a private room, an entire bar, or a penthouse, you need to go over every detail with the manager or owner. Be business savvy and get everything you agree upon in writing, including the food and drink menus. A contract also eliminates any last-minute charges or hidden costs that weren't mentioned up front; you only have to pay for what is on that signed piece of paper. Don't let money matters give you a case of the post-party blues. Here's what you need to consider: Is there a fee for renting a private room? Do you have to guarantee that a certain number of people will show up, and if they don't, are you required to pay for the empty places? If it's part of the venue's policy, try to wiggle your way out. Who wants to pay for that friend who always flakes?

If the space is not exclusively yours, make sure you can reserve tables. Are the valet, coat check, hostess, and security included in the room fee? How many servers will be made available to your group? If you need more, how much will it cost? One server for every six people is the ideal spread, since it ensures that everyone gets attended to efficiently. Is there a DJ? If not, can you bring your own? Does the venue have a sound system? Will you be able to play your own mix of CDs?

Be sure to get all the details on how the venue will charge for cocktails. Is it per person, per hour, or based on how much your partygoers drink? Are top-shelf liquors included? Decide which method of drink service is best for you: an open bar, bottle service (in which you pick your preferred brand of liquor and set it on tables in buckets of ice along with mixers and garnishes), or a cash bar. Work out the best deal possible. This may mean having an open bar for a set period of time and then, later in the evening, switching to cash. Also ask if the venue is willing to serve nonalcoholic drinks gratis. And not just bottled water; having coffee, cappuccino, and espresso free of charge is an added bonus.

Is décor provided by the venue? If so, ask if it includes tables, flowers, centerpieces, table linens, extra seating, and so on. Or find out if you can bring your own décor.

Can you have your own doorperson? If not, be certain that the bouncer has a list of your guests so they don't have any problem getting in.

Money, Money, Money

Not a mathlete? No problem—we've made it easy for you to figure out your budget. With proper planning, a dinner party can cost half as much as it would without good planning. And don't forget to count all those little things that often add up to beaucoup bucks, like tax, extra film, and last-minute purchases. We've put together a detailed list of everything you need to think about when figuring your budget. It doesn't take a math whiz, so whip out that calculator and get going!

Of course, you won't need every single item for every single party, but there are some items that come standard, like invites. Regardless, photocopy the next pages or retype it to suit your needs.

Item	Estimated	Actual
Invitations		
Save-the-date cards		
Stationery (boxed, custom-made, or homemade)		
Lettering (professional calligraphy, the services of an art student or a handwriting specialist, dinner for a friend who did you a favor and wrote the invitations for you)		
Printing or **photocopying**		
Labels		
Stuffing		
Sealing		
Mailing (stamps, a messenger service, or hand delivery)		
Location		
Home or **another venue**		
Room or **venue rental** charge		
Plating charge (if you bring your own cake to a restaurant)		
Corkage fee (if you BYOB)		
Tipping for all servers		
Tax		
Dining Necessities		
Plates		
Utensils		
Tabletop items like **napkins, linens, serving dishes, and trays** (Some of which you may need to rent or purchase.)		
Drinks		
Alcohol (wine, champagne, hard alcohol, and after-dinner drinks)		
Mixers		
Soda		
Water		
Cups (glass, paper, or plastic)		
Condiments (olives, cherries, and lemons)		
Ice		
Shakers and other **bar items**, such as coolers		
Coffee and tea		
Staff		
Chef and chef's **assistants**		
Waiters		
Bartenders		
Bar backers		

Item	Estimated	Actual
Busboys		
Doorman (even if you're giving thirty dollars to that big burly dude your friend is friends with)		
Check-in attendants		
Coat check		
Valet		
Bathroom attendant		
Entertainment (a psychic, a live band, a henna painter, a tattoo artist, strippers, dancers, or a body piercer—hey, you never know!)		
Cleanup (Someone's got to deal with the mess.)		
Décor		
Place cards		
Food stylist		
Décor designer		
Lighting (candles, lightbulbs, and spotlights)		
Sound (a DJ, sound equipment, a CD player, or live music)		
Flowers (hiring a florist or hitting the flower mart)		
Rentals (furniture, glasses, a coat rack, and/or a tent)		
Other decorations (centerpieces and napkin holders)		
Miscellaneous		
Security		
Insurance		
Permits		
Space heaters or heat lamps		
Fans		
Extra toilet paper		
Garbage bags		
Napkins		
Photographer		
Extra film		
Disposable cameras for the tables		
Video crew		
Gift bags		
TOTAL		

REMEMBER:
Always calculate the **estimated** versus **actual cost**.
Keep every **receipt**.
Overestimate by 10 percent for unexpected costs.

recipes

ORGANICALLY GOOD

Elixir Tonics VirtualBliss

2 ounces pineapple juice
2 ounces lime juice
1 squirt Elixir Virtual Buddha tonic
Garnish

Pour all of the liquid ingredients into a chimney glass. Stir and garnish.

Serves 1

Recipe courtesy of Elixir Tonics & Teas

WHAT IS YOUR FAVORITE DRINK AT A PARTY?

"Martinis." **—Nicky Hilton**

"Mixed martinis, margaritas, and mojitos." **—Molly Sims**

"Champagne with fresh apple juice." **—Venus Williams**

"I like to spike punch." **—David Arquette**

"Shots of tequila." **—Rita Schrager**

"Ketel One on the rocks." **—Michael Kors**

"Patrón on the rocks, with lime." **—Bijou Phillips**

"I like to drink cranberry with lime juice and sparkling water. That's what I drink when I am not in the mood to have alcohol. Or a good glass of wine. I like Battard Montrachet." **—Forest Whitaker**

"Strawberry margaritas with Pátron or Corzo" **—Stephen Dorff**

OH, SUGAR!

Serena's Grand Slam Punch

750-liter bottle Grey Goose vodka
3.25 liters Courvoisier cognac
8 ounces peach schnapps
3 bottles Rose's Cocktail Infusions Blue Raspberry
Ice

Mix all liquid ingredients in a large punch bowl. Then pour over ice.

Serves many!

Recipe courtesy of Anastasia Williams of Anastasia's Catering

Corzo Cooler

2 parts Corzo Silver tequila
2 parts pineapple juice
Dash Chambord
Ice
Soda
Sliced pineapple, for garnish

Mix the tequila, pineapple juice, and Chambord. Serve on the rocks and top the drink with soda. Garnish with a pineapple slice.

Recipe courtesy of Corzo tequila

SITARS AND SAMOSAS

Raj's Cocktail

1 fresh mango, sliced
1/3 cup Grey Goose vodka
1/3 cup San Pellegrino sparkling water
1/3 cup fresh lime juice

Combine all of the ingredients in a blender. Blend for 3 minutes and serve.

Serves 2

Recipe courtesy of Raj Kanodia, M.D

Alana Stewart's Best Cosmo in the World

3 ounces Grey Goose L'Orange vodka
1/2 ounce Cointreau
1 ounce cranberry juice
Squeeze of lime

Serves 1

Recipe courtesy of Alana Stewart

Grey Goose Vanilla Gingersnap

2 ounces Grey Goose La Vanille vodka
Ice
1/2 ounce ginger ale

Chill the vodka over ice in a cocktail shaker. Strain into a martini glass. Top with the ginger ale. To serve, garnish the martini glass with a cocktail charm.

Serves 1

Recipe courtesy of Kathleen Sacchi, The Fine Art of Catering

Strawberry Nectar Tropical Punch

1 pint mango juice
1 pint strawberry juice
1 quart sparkling mineral water
Ice
4–6 nasturtium flowers (or seasonal flowers of choice)
12 lime wedges, for garnish

Pour the mango juice, strawberry juice, and sparkling mineral water into a punch bowl. Stir to make a frothy punch. Add the ice. Float the flowers in the punch and serve in punch glasses. Garnish each glass with a lime wedge.

Serves 12

Recipe courtesy of Kathleen Sacchi, The Fine Art of Catering

AFTERNOON SPLASH

Pink Creamsicle

2 ounces Grey Goose vodka
1 ounce amaretto
1 scoop strawberry ice cream
1 ounce half-and-half
3 ounces peach puree
1 fresh strawberry, for garnish

Mix the vodka, amaretto, ice cream, half-and-half, and peach puree in a blender. Serve in a hurricane glass. Garnish with the fresh strawberry.

Serves 1

Recipe courtesy of Kathleen Sacchi, The Fine Art of Catering

Minty Gimlet

Infused simple syrup
1 cup sugar
1 cup boiling water
5 sprigs fresh mint
1/4 cup Rose's lime juice
Juice of 1 lemon
Gimlet
2 ounces Grey Goose vodka
Ice
1 Mint sprig, for garnish

For simple syrup:
• Dissolve the sugar in the boiling water. Add the fresh mint, the Rose's lime juice, and the lemon juice. Simmer for 5 minutes. Pour the mixture through a strainer to separate the mint particles.
• Cool to room temperature.
• Yields 15 servings of syrup

For gimlet:
Straight up: Chill the vodka in an iced cocktail shaker. Add 1/2 ounce infused simple syrup. Shake well and strain into a martini glass. Garnish with the mint sprig.
On the rocks: Fill a rocks glass with ice. Pour the vodka. Add 1/2 ounce infused simple syrup. Garnish with the mint sprig.

Serves 1

Recipe courtesy of Kathleen Sacchi, The Fine Art of Catering

FOR THE TWEETY BIRDS

The Tweety

2 ounces Grey Goose Le Citron vodka
Sour mix
1 lemon wedge, for garnish

Pour the vodka into an iced cocktail shaker. Add two splashes of sour mix. Shake well. Strain into a martini glass, garnish with the lemon wedge, and serve straight up.

Serves 1

Recipe courtesy of Kathleen Sacchi, The Fine Art of Catering

The Puddy Tat

Ice
8 ounces Kahlua
4 ounces half-and-half

Fill a cocktail shaker with ice. Add the Kahlua and the half-and-half. Shake well. Strain into martini glasses and serve straight up.

Serves 3

Recipe courtesy of Kathleen Sacchi, The Fine Art of Catering

"Serve a theme drink or drinks and offer them to guests as they arrive. For instance, if it's summer, serve peach, watermelon, as well as regular margaritas. Or serve peach or lychee martinis. During the holidays, serve cosmos and green-apple martinis. Have a good assortment of liquor and wine as well, for those who don't want the special drink." **— Alana Stewart**

PARTY PRINCESS

Serendipity 3's Secret Frrrozen Hot Chocolate

1 1/2 level teaspoons each of sweetened Van Houton cocoa and Droste cocoa
1 1/2 teaspoons sugar
1 tablespoon unsalted butter
1/2 ounce each of the following chocolates: Callebaut, Valrhona, Lindt, Cadbury, Anton Berg, Freia, Marabu, Ghirardelli, and Cacao Barry
1/2 pint of milk
1/2 quart crushed ice
Whipped cream
Grated chocolate

In the top of a double boiler over boiling water, melt the cocoa with the sugar and butter, creaming them into a smooth paste. Add the chocolate and continue melting, slowly dribbling in half the milk while stirring. Cool to room temperature. Place the remaining cup of milk, the room temperature chocolate mixture, and ice in a blender. Blend on high speed until smooth and the consistency of a frozen daiquiri. Pour into a giant goblet and top with whipped cream and chocolate shavings. Enjoy with a spoon or a straw...or both!

NOTE: You can also buy the premade packets at Serendipity's or Williams-Sonoma.

Serves 1

Recipe courtesy of *Sweet Serendipity: Delicious Desserts and Devilish Dish* by Stephen Bruce with Brett Bara (Universe).

LET THE FUR FLY!

Stephen Dorff's Frozen Margarita

6 ounces Margaritaville Margarita Mix
2 ounces Corzo tequila
1 cup fresh strawberries
2 tablespoons Rose's lime juice
1/4 cup sugar
2 Lime wedges, for garnish (Sliced fruit is also an option.)
Kosher salt
1/2 cups ice

Combine the Margaritaville Margarita Mix, tequila, strawberries, lime juice, and sugar in a Waring Pro blender for 3 minutes. Rub the rim of a margarita glass with a lime wedge and then dust it with kosher salt. Stir the blended ingredients with the ice and pour the liquid into the glass, with or without ice. Garnish with a lime wedge and/or sliced fruit.

Serves 2

Recipe courtesy of Stephen Dorff

POKER PARTY

The Whiskey Blue Flirtini

1 1/2 ounces Vox
1 ounce pineapple juice
Champagne
Cherry

Combine Vox and pineapple juice, and finish with champagne to taste. Garnish with a cherry.

Serves 1

Recipe courtesy of Whiskey Blue

David Copperfield's Black Magic Martini

3/4 ounce Grey Goose vodka
1/4 ounce black sambuca
1/4 ounce Goldschläger cinnamon schnapps
Ice
1 cinnamon stick, for garnish

Combine the vodka, sambuca, and schnapps in a shaker with ice and mix. Strain into a chilled martini glass. Garnish with the cinnamon stick.

Serves 1

Recipe courtesy of David Copperfield

El Tiempo's Michelada

18 ounces V8 juice
6 ounces Valentina Salsa Picante Mexican hot sauce
6 ounces fresh-squeezed lime juice
2 ounces Tabasco sauce
1 teaspoon salt
Salt for rimming glasses
1 bottle Mexican beer
14–16 lime wedges for garnish

Stir the tomato juice, salsa, lime juice, Tabasco sauce, and salt into a one-quart container. Mix well. Chill in the refrigerator. When the mix has cooled, salt the rims (optional) of chilled collins glasses and pour 2 ounces of the mix into each glass. Add ice-cold Mexican beer and mix well. Serve each drink with a lime garnish.

Serves 14–16

Recipe courtesy of El Tiempo Cantina, Houston, Texas

Marquee's Razz Delight

2 ounces raspberry vodka
6 ounces Schweppes tonic water
Splash cranberry juice
Lime wheel
10-ounce highball glass
Ice

Combine raspberry vodka, Schweppes tonic water, and a splash of cranberry juice in a small shaker. Shake for a few seconds. Pour into a highball glass filled with ice and garnish with a fresh lime wheel and a straw.

Serves 1

Recipe courtesy of Marquee nightclub

Shareef's Fabulous Mojito Martini Champagne

2 lime wedges
3–5 mint sprigs
1 tablespoon sugar
2 dashes sour mix
Enough ice to fill a tall glass
1 ounce Malibu rum
1 ounce Bacardi Limón rum
Splash of Moët & Chandon Nectar Impérial
Fresh mint leaves and 1 lime wedge, for garnish

Combine the lime wedges, mint, sugar, and sour mix in a tall glass and muddle all the ingredients. Fill the glass with ice. Add the Malibu and Bacardi Limón rum and a splash of Moët & Chandon Nectar Impérial. Stir, and pour into a chilled martini glass. Garnish with the fresh mint leaves and wedge of lime.

Serves 1

Recipe courtesy of the Forge, Miami Beach, Florida

Michael Michele's White Chocolate Martini

Godiva White Chocolate liquor
Vanilla Grey Goose vodka
Shaved dark chocolate
Shaker with ice

Mix one shot of Godiva liquor and one shot of vanilla vodka. People should adjust the amount to their particular taste. (I often allow the ice to melt a bit, therefore watering down the liquor (for those who like less). Some people prefer a stronger drink, others don't.

Shake with ice in shaker. I wrap a towel around the shaker, to create the absolute COLDEST drink possible.

Shave dark chocolate on the top. Shave the chocolate into very FINE shavings. Pour into a beautiful crystal glass and TOAST!

Serve with a tray of chocolates.

Serves 2

Recipe courtesy of Michael Michele

The Whiskey Blue Tropical Martini

2 ounces Bacardi Cóco
1 ounce Midori
1 ounce pineapple juice

Serves 1

Recipe courtesy of Whiskey Blue

The Divorce Cocktail

2 ounces Grey Goose original vodka
Dash of vermouth

Shake or stir on ice.
Garnish with an olive or a twist.
Serve in martini glass.

Serves 1

Recipe courtesy of Kathleen Sacchi, The Fine Art of Catering

The Pink Lady

2 ounces Grey Goose L' Orange
1/2 ounce sweet-and-sour mix
1 ounce cranberry juice

Shake and serve in martini glass.
Garnished with lime twist.

Serves 1

Recipe courtesy of Kathleen Sacchi, The Fine Art of Catering

Nobu's Passion Fruit Sake

1.9 quarts sake (junmai)
1 1/2 pounds passion fruit puree
2 1/3 tablespoons simple syrup

Mix all ingredients and serve chilled.

Serves a lot

Recipe courtesy of Nobu Restaurant

For the Love of Vanilla Creme

2 ounces Grey Goose Le Vanille
2 ounces ginger ale

Served over ice in a rocks glass

Serves 1

Recipe courtesy of Lara Shriftman

Malibu Splash

1 ounce Grey Goose Le Citron
1 ounce Blue Caracoa
1/2 ounce grapefruit juice
1/2 ounce sugar

Shake with ice and serve in martini glass. Garnish with a cherry.

Serves 1

Recipe courtesy of Maeve Quinlan

IT'S A PLEASURE DOING BUSINESS

Paris's Crimson Champagne Cocktail

BRANDY-CRANBERRY SYRUP
1 quart cranberry juice cocktail
4 slices fresh ginger
1 cinnamon stick
1 piece star anise

Yields 10 servings of syrup

CHAMPAGNE COCKTAIL
1/4 cup brandy
Champagne
1 fresh cranberry, for garnish

For cranberry syrup:
In a medium saucepan, boil the cranberry juice cocktail, the ginger, the cinnamon stick, and the star anise for half an hour or until reduced to 1 cup. Let cool.

For cocktail:
Fill a champagne flute half-full with champagne and add the brandy. Add 1 ounce Brandy-Cranberry Syrup and mix. Garnish with the fresh cranberry.

Serves 1

Recipe courtesy of Kathleen Sacchi, The Fine Art of Catering

The Privé Kiss

2 ounces Grey Goose vodka
1/2 ounce cranberry juice
1/2 ounce pineapple juice
Splash of Perrier Jouët champagne
1 fresh lemon wedge, for garnish

Pour the vodka, cranberry juice, and pineapple juice into a mixing tin. Shake, and strain the liquid into a martini glass. Top the glass with a splash of champagne and garnish with the lemon wedge.

Serves 1

Recipe courtesy of the Opium Group

WHAT IS YOUR FAVORITE DRINK RECIPE?

"Caipirinhas, a drink from Brazil made with lime and Brazilian sugarcane vodka. I served it at a toga party I had one year and everyone ended up in the pool!"
— **Alexandra von Furstenberg**

"Peach martinis. Make them with fresh nectar juice and two slices of peach on top. And frozen margaritas—put half a shot of Corzo on top of a drink that is already made."
— **Maeve Quinlan**

"For a good drink, find a great bartender." — **Sarah Michelle Gellar**

WHAT IS YOUR FAVORITE PARTY MENU?

"I always enjoy a barbecue party. You can cook a lot of food in a quick amount of time, and in a pinch you can throw a couple of hot dogs and hamburgers on the grill. Steaks cook quickly on a grill. Experiment to find the perfect barbecue sauce, because I will not share my secret."
— **David Arquette**

"I particularly like soul food, since I'm from Texas." — **Alana Stewart**

"Nothing messy, nothing smelly, and everything too fattening."
— **Michael Michele**

"Sushi—it's easy to eat and won't get on your dress."
— **Sarah Michelle Gellar**

"Mexican tacos!" — **Paulina Rubio**

"Finger food—pizza, mozzarella sticks, chicken fingers."
— **Nicky Hilton**

"Pure indulgence: mounds of Beluga caviar and toast points. Or great comfort foods: mini grilled-cheese sandwiches and burgers finished off with ice-cream sandwiches."
— **Michael Kors**

"I don't like to serve anything too complicated. Something tasty like a combination of fish and chicken. Just wholesome, good-tasting food."
— **Alexandra von Furstenberg**

"Bite-size is key!"
— **Maeve Quinlan and Jennifer Finnigan**

"Munchies, munchies, and more munchies!"
— **Lara Flynn Boyle**

For icing
- Mix ingredients and spread over warm cake. Place under broiler until icing turns light brown (watch it closely).
- Cut bars into small squares and serve for finger food at the party.

Recipe courtesy of Dani Janssen

Alana Stewart's Lemon Pie

CRUST
1 1/4 cup graham cracker crumbs
1/2 cup ginger snap crumbs
1 stick butter, melted
1/2 cup sugar

FILLING
2 cans sweetened condensed milk
1/4 cup fresh lemon or lime or Key lime juice
3 egg yolks

MERINGUE
4 or 5 egg whites
1/4 cup sugar

For crust:
- Preheat oven to 375 degrees.
- Mix ingredients and press into pie pan; bake 10 minutes at 375 degrees.

For filling:
Mix ingredients well. Fill cooled crust.

For meringue:
- Preheat oven to 350 degrees.
- Beat egg whites until stiff, add sugar, and beat until glossy. Put meringue on top of pie and bake 10 minutes (or until meringue is lightly browned) at 350 degrees.

Recipe courtesy of Alana Stewart

WHAT IS YOUR FAVORITE DESSERT?

"I always serve more than one dessert, which I make myself. Lemon or Key lime pie, peach cobbler, cookies 'n' cream cheesecake, killer brownies, and some assorted homemade cookies." — **Alana Stewart**

"I'm a cake-and-ice-cream guy, and it doesn't have to be a birthday." — **David Arquette**

"Chocolate-covered strawberries—it is a timeless dessert." — **Sarah Michelle Gellar**

"Anything made from chocolate. I love melted chocolate cake served warm." — **Forest Whitaker**

"I have a stellar recipe for *very rich* cheesecake. It is always a major winner." — **Jackie Collins**

"Chocolate soufflé or my mom's red velvet cake. The red velvet cake can also be made into cupcakes." —**Molly Sims**

Jackie Collins's Hollyrich Cheesecake

CHEESECAKE
16 of your favorite cookies
3/4 cup of sugar, divided
1/4 pound unsalted butter, melted
1 pound whipped cream cheese
2 teaspoons vanilla

1/2 cup cream
1 cup sour cream
2 eggs, beaten

TOPPING
1 cup sour cream
1 tablespoon sugar
1 teaspoon vanilla

- Preheat oven to 450 degrees.
- Crunch cookies together until they make crumbs. Mix them with 1/4 cup of the sugar and melted butter. Press mixture into sides and bottom of a buttered pie pan, 8 or 10 inches, and bake at 450 degrees for 5 minutes.
- The filling is made by combining whipped cream cheese with the vanilla, cream, sour cream, and remaining 1/2 cup sugar. Add eggs and mix very thoroughly. Pour mixture into crust and bake for 20 minutes at 350 degrees.
- When you remove pie from oven, cover it with sour cream, sugar, and vanilla topping.
- After adding topping, bake another 5 minutes, and cool before serving.

Serves 6–8

Recipe courtesy of Jackie Collins

Anastasia Williams's Peach Cobbler

2 tablespoons flour
1 cup water or syrup from 1 can of peaches
1 cup brown sugar, plus extra for sprinkling
2 cups granulated sugar
1 cup butter
1/4 cup vanilla flavoring

4 tablespoons cinnamon, plus extra for sprinkling
2 tablespoons flour
3 Pillsbury piecrusts
4 cups peeled (if fresh), sliced peaches, fresh or canned
1/2 stick butter, sliced

- In a saucepan over low heat, mix flour with water (if using fresh peaches) or syrup (if using canned peaches). Add brown and granulated sugars, butter, vanilla, and cinnamon to saucepan.
- Take 1 piecrust and place it in a 6-inch pie pan. Lightly brown piecrust in oven.
- Layer peaches over browned crust and cover them with sauce mixture.
- Take second and third crusts and lightly brown them in oven.
- Crumble crusts and spread crumbs over top of peaches. Sprinkle brown sugar and cinnamon and sparingly place slices of butter on top of crumbs.
- Bake at 350 degrees for 30 minutes.

Serves 10–15

Recipe courtesy of Anastasia Williams of Anastasia's Catering

Joe's Famous Key Lime Pie

CRUST
1 cup plus 2 1/2 tablespoons crumbled graham crackers
1/3 cup sugar
5 tablespoons unsalted butter, melted

FILLING
3 egg yolks
1 1/2 teaspoons grated lime zest
1 14-ounce can sweetened condensed milk
2/3 cup freshly squeezed lime juice
1 cup heavy cream, chilled
1 tablespoon confectioners' sugar

For crust:
• Preheat oven to 350 degrees. Butter a 9-inch pie pan. Put graham crackers in a medium-sized bowl and mix in sugar. When blended, add melted butter and mix until combined. Press mixture into bottom and sides of pie pan. Bake for 8 minutes, or until crust is golden.
• Set aside. Leave oven on.

For filling:
• In a medium-sized bowl, beat egg yolks and lime zest with an electric mixer on high until very fluffy, about 5 minutes.
• Gradually add condensed milk and beat until thick, 3 or 4 minutes. Lower mixer speed to medium and slowly add lime juice, mixing until just combined. Pour into pie shell and bake for 10 minutes, or until center is set. Allow to cool, then refrigerate until chilled, about 2 hours.
• Whip cream and confectioners' sugar until nearly stiff.
• To serve, slice pie into wedges and dollop with whipped cream.

NOTE: You can also order the pies and have them Fed Exed.

Makes a 9-inch pie

Recipe courtesy of Joe's Stone Crab

Bombay Café's Jalpari Tikka with Mint Chutney

FISH
1 2-inch piece fresh ginger, peeled and coarsely chopped
6 cloves garlic, peeled and coarsely chopped
2 green serrano chilis
1 tablespoon ground coriander
1 teaspoon ground cumin
1 teaspoon cayenne
1 cup yogurt
1 1/2 teaspoon ajwain seeds (available in Indian markets)
2 pounds Chilean sea bass or halibut, cut into 2-inch cubes
1 1/2 teaspoons sea salt
Juice of 1 lemon
1 tablespoon vegetable oil
2 medium yellow onions, peeled and cut into quarters
1 large red pepper, cut into 2-inch squares
2 firm tomatoes, cut into quarters
Lemon wedges for garnish

MINT CHUTNEY
1 small onion, quartered
2–3 serrano green chilis (depending on how hot you like it)*
2 small cloves garlic
1/2 cup cilantro (do not use the tough stems)
1 1/2 cups tightly packed mint leaves
1 teaspoon cumin seeds, dry-roasted and ground*
3/4 teaspoon salt
Juice of 1 1/2 limes

For fish:
• Puree ginger, garlic, green chilis, coriander, cumin, and cayenne with yogurt. Add ajwain seeds to puree and mix well. Set aside.
• Place fish in a large bowl and season with salt and lemon juice. Add marinade and mix to coat well. Add oil and again mix to coat well.
• Thread fish, onions, pepper, and tomatoes onto metal skewers or wooden skewers that have been soaked in water for a few hours.
• Barbecue, broil, or grill fish in a stovetop griddle pan with ridges. Cook 3 to 4 minutes on each side until fish is firm to the touch.

For chutney:
• Put onion, chilis, and garlic in a blender jar and puree using a little water to a fine paste.
• Add rest of ingredients, add a little more water as needed, and blend to form thick sauce.
• Adjust salt, lime, and chilis to taste.
• Remove to a bowl for serving. (Yields approximately 1 cup.)
• Remove fish to a serving platter, garnish with lemon wedges, and serve with a small bowl of Mint Chutney.

Serves 8

Recipe courtesy of the Bombay Café

Mini Monte Cristo Sandwiches

8 slices white sandwich bread
8 tablespoons Dijonnaise
4 ounces thinly sliced imported
Swiss cheese
4 ounces sliced turkey
4 ounces thinly sliced Black
Forest ham

4 eggs
1/2 cup milk
Salt and pepper
1 tablespoon butter
Powdered sugar
1/2 cup raspberry jam

• Spread each slice of bread with one tablespoon of Dijonnaise. Top each slice of bread with 1 slice of cheese. Top 4 slices of bread with 1 ounce each of turkey and ham, and cover with remaining slices of bread and cheese.
• Beat eggs with milk, salt, and pepper. Dip each sandwich into egg batter as if it were French toast.
• Melt butter in a sauté pan or on a griddle on medium-low heat. Cook each sandwich until golden brown on each side and cheese is melted. Cut each sandwich into 4 triangles and then cut each triangle in half.
• Sprinkle with powdered sugar and serve with small bowl of raspberry jam.

Makes 32 mini sandwiches

Recipe courtesy of Kathleen Sacchi, The Fine Art of Catering

Mommer's Bellinia

18 slices Pepperidge Farm Cinnamon Swirl bread (no raisins)
3 eggs
1/4 cup water

3 containers soft cream cheese, room temperature
Sugar
Lemon juice

• Preheat oven to 375 degrees.
• Roll slices of bread out with a rolling pin. Beat eggs with a fork and add water. Soak each piece of bread in egg mixture. Put cream cheese on half of each slice with sugar and a drop of lemon juice. Fold each slice in half and cut end crusts off, then cut each folded slice into 2 triangles.
• Bake in a foil pan until brown at 375 degrees. Serve it warm.

Makes 36 appetizer pieces

Recipe courtesy of Lara's grandmother Mommer

Cage-Free Deviled Eggs

12 cage-free eggs
1/2 cup mayonnaise
1 teaspoons Dijon mustard
Salt and pepper
3 tablespoons minced chives

• Place eggs in medium saucepan and cover with cold water. Bring to a boil and cook for 2 minutes. Turn off heat and cover pot. Let sit for 10 minutes.
• Drain eggs and peel immediately under cold running water. Chill eggs and cut in half lengthwise. Remove egg yolks and place in small bowl. Add remaining ingredients (except chives) to yolks and mash with fork until smooth. Fill hollow of egg whites with yolk mixture and sprinkle with chives. Chill until time to serve.

Makes 24 deviled eggs

Recipe courtesy of Kathleen Sacchi, The Fine Art of Catering

Peter's Chic Split de Banane

1 banana, sliced in two lengthwise
2 tablespoons simple syrup
1 scoop each coffee, chocolate, and strawberry gelato
2 tablespoons chocolate ganache
2 tablespoons toasted walnuts

Grill sliced banana in simple syrup till golden brown. Plate it and add scoops of coffee, chocolate, and strawberry gelato. Top with chocolate ganache and toasted walnuts.

Serves 1

Recipe courtesy of Peter Som

Mini Grilled Cheese

2 slices thin-sliced white
Pepperidge Farm bread
1 slice Kraft Singles American
cheese
1 tablespoon butter

- Assemble the sandwich (cheese and bread).
- Melt butter in a nonstick pan. Slide sandwich into butter and brown on each side. (For best results, cook on low heat so cheese has time to melt and you can control how brown you want the toast.) Cut into 4 triangles or squares and serve.

Serves 1

Recipe courtesy of Cary Richardson, Cary Cooks, Inc.

Pop Burger's Mini Hamburgers

HAMBURGERS	6 teaspoons Pop Burger Sauce
6 small round brioche rolls	(recipe follows)
Salt and fresh-ground black	**POP BURGER SAUCE**
pepper	1/2 cup mayonnaise
6 2-ounce ground chuck	1/4 cup ketchup
patties	1 tablespoon fresh lime juice
3 slices good-quality American	1 teaspoon hot sauce
cheese, cut in half	2 tablespoons chopped pickles
12 slices ripe roma tomatoes	Salt and fresh-ground black
6 tablespoons shredded ro-	pepper
maine lettuce	

- Toast rolls in warm nonstick skillet.
- Char-grill burgers that have been seasoned with salt and fresh-ground black pepper. Top burgers with cheese and tomato slices for final minute of cooking time (3 to 4 minutes total).
Spread roll bottoms with Pop Burger Sauce and top with shredded lettuce, burger, tomato, cheese, and roll tops.

Serves 3 (2 per person)

Recipes courtesy of Pop Burger

Pigs in a Blanket

1 package Hillshire Farm Lit'l Smokies cocktail links
(about 48)
1 package Pepperidge Farm puff pastry sheets
1 egg white
Flour for dusting pastry

- Preheat oven to 375 degrees.
- Drain cocktail wieners on a paper towel. Roll out puff pastry dough on a floured cutting board and cut dough into long strips. The width of the strips should be equal to the length of a cocktail wiener. Wrap puff pastry around each wiener to just cover (seams meet). Brush each one with egg white.
- Place wieners on parchment-covered cookie sheet and bake at 375 degrees for about 20 to 25 minutes, or until pastry is puffed up and cooked through.
- Serve with a bowl of your favorite mustard.

Makes about 48 pieces

Recipe courtesy of Cary Richardson, Cary Cooks, Inc.

WHAT IS YOUR FAVORITE PARTY MENU?

"Lots of canapés based on favorites—nothing too precious or fancy. Mini-hamburgers or mini new potatoes with crème fraîche and caviar. Believe me, *everything* tastes amazing when it's wrapped with bacon and thrown under the broiler for a minute."　**—Peter Som**

"A kids' menu."　**—Rita Schrager**

Dorothy Sims's Red Velvet Cake

1/2 cup shortening	2 1/2 cups flour
1 1/2 cups sugar	1 teaspoon vanilla
2 eggs	1 cup buttermilk
2 tablespoons cocoa	1 teaspoon soda
1 1/2 ounces red food coloring	1 tablespoon vinegar
1 teaspoon salt	

- Preheat oven to 350 degrees.
- Cream shortening; beat in sugar gradually. Add eggs, one at a time, beating well after each addition. Make a paste of cocoa and food coloring in a separate bowl; add to creamed mixture. Add salt, flour, and vanilla alternately with buttermilk, beating well after each addition.
- Sprinkle soda over vinegar, pour vinegar over batter. Stir until thoroughly mixed.
- Bake in 3 8-inch pans or 2 9-inch pans for 30 minute at 350 degrees.

NOTE: To make cupcakes, divide batter into cupcake tins. Bake for about 20 minutes at 350 degrees, or until wooden skewer comes out clean.

Makes 1 cake or 12–16 cupcakes

Recipe courtesy of Molly Sims

WHAT DO YOU CONSIDER THE BEST PARTY MUSIC?

"Best music for a party is upbeat music that you can dance to." —**Kristin Cavallari**

"Old Madonna and Michael Jackson." —**Nicky Hilton**

"Latin music." —**Rita Schrager**

"Classic Donna Summer or Barry White for a big-energy party." —**Michael Kors**

"Seventies funk never goes out of style. A little disco sprinkled in. The occasional '70s rock ballad, for good measure." —**David Arquette**

"If you're having a dinner party at home, I love to play Wideawake, Iron and Wine, Ryan Adams, The Killers, Coldplay, and Snow Patrol. If you're having a party at a club, the best idea is to get a DJ and trust that they're musical geniuses! I love DJ AM and Samantha Ronson." —**Molly Sims**

"Frank Sinatra and Bobby Darin are great for dinner parties and any place where a straight-up martini can be found. My husband has recently discovered music from Senegal, which is mellow and gorgeous and has a great beat." —**Gigi Levangie Grazer**

"I love Dean Martin and Frank Sinatra. It reminds me of older Hollywood." —**Sarah Michelle Gellar**

"*Exile on Main Street* by the Rolling Stones, made while the band was living in a house in the south of France having a month-long party. Nothing else comes close." —**Luke Wilson**

"Open forum! A mixture of hip-hop, rock, '80s, and '70s!" —**Venus Williams**

"Bossa nova or hip-hop; it depends. I love to dance. I think everyone has more fun if the music makes them wanna move." —**Bijou Phillips**

"I can't narrow it down. Depends on your guests and your theme." —**Regina King**

"Disco. Earth, Wind and Fire, Kool and the Gang, Gloria Gaynor, old school disco." —**Allison Sarofim**

"Old school always does the trick. There is something familiar about it and it puts people at ease." —**Forest Whitaker**

Taverna Tony's Tzatziki

2 cucumbers (peeled, seeded, and diced)
3 cups Greek yogurt (or any good, thick yogurt), drained of its water in a cheesecloth for 12 hours
2 large garlic cloves, crushed and finely diced
1 teaspoon fresh mint, finely chopped
1 teaspoon fresh dill, finely chopped
Salt and pepper
Virgin olive oil
Fresh chopped parsley

• Warm pita bread or fresh toasted bread
• Mix first six ingredients in a bowl and sprinkle with olive oil and parsley. Serve on warm pita bread or toast.

Serves 8

Recipe courtesy of Taverna Tony

Lara Flynn Boyle's Puppy Chow

9 cups Chex cereal (any variety)
1 cup semisweet chocolate and white chocolate chips
1/2 cup creamy peanut butter
1/4 cup margarine or butter
1 1/2 cups powdered sugar

Pour cereal into large bowl. Melt chocolate chips, peanut butter, and margarine or butter on the stove on low heat, stirring frequently, or in the microwave in a microwavable bowl on high for 1 minute or until mixture is smooth and creamy. Remove from heat/microwave. Pour mixture over cereal and mix until cereal is covered. Pour cereal mixture into a plastic storage container and shake to ensure that cereal is evenly coated. Pour cereal mixture onto waxed paper and place in refrigerator to harden. Pour cereal mixture into individual serving bowls and sprinkle with powdered sugar.

Serves 10–20

Recipe courtesy of Lara Flynn Boyle

Makes a great appetizer or dessert

California Pizza Kitchen's Spinach-Artichoke Dip

1/4 cup olive oil
2 tablespoons unsalted butter
3/4 cup diced white or yellow onion (1/8-inch dice)
1 1/2 tablespoons minced garlic
1/2 cup all-purpose flour
1 1/2 cups chicken stock (preferably homemade)
1 1/2 cups heavy cream
3/4 cup freshly grated Parmesan cheese
2 tablespoons dehydrated chicken stock base or crumbed bouillon cubes
1 1/2 tablespoons freshly squeezed lemon juice
1 teaspoon sugar
3/4 cup sour cream
12 ounces frozen spinach, defrosted, drained, wrung out by hand, and coarsely chopped
6 ounces canned artichoke bottoms, drained and cut into 1/4-inch slices
1 cup finely shredded Monterey Jack cheese
3/4 teaspoon Tabasco sauce
Blue and white corn tortilla chips

• In a large saucepan, warm olive oil and butter together over medium heat. When butter has melted, add onion and cook, stirring occasionally, until the onion is wilted, 3 to 4 minutes. Stir in garlic and cook 2 to 3 minutes longer, stirring frequently and stopping before onion and garlic brown.
• Sprinkle flour and continue cooking, stirring continuously, until mixture turns a golden blond color, 10 to 15 minutes. Then, whisking continuously, slowly pour in stock until it is smoothly incorporated. When mixture begins to simmer, stir in cream. Let it return to a simmer. Remove from heat, add Parmesan, chicken base or bouillon cubes, lemon juice, and sugar, and stir until thoroughly blended.
• Add sour cream, spinach, artichoke bottoms, Monterey Jack cheese, and Tabasco sauce, and stir until ingredients are thoroughly combined and cheese has melted. Transfer to a warmed serving bowl and serve immediately, accompanied by blue and white corn tortilla chips.

Serves 8–10

Recipe courtesy of California Pizza Kitchen, Inc.

California Pizza Kitchen's BBQ Chopped-Chicken Salad

FRIED TORTILLA STRIPS
Vegetable oil for deep frying
12 corn tortillas cut in 1/4-inch-wide strips
GARDEN HERB RANCH DRESSING
1/2 teaspoon dry mustard
1/4 teaspoon cold water
2 3/4 cups mayonnaise
1 cup buttermilk
7 tablespoons sour cream
2 1/2 tablespoons apple cider vinegar
1 1/2 tablespoons thinly sliced scallions (greens and whites)
2 teaspoons minced garlic
2 teaspoons minced fresh Italian parsley
1 1/2 teaspoons Worcestershire sauce
1 teaspoon minced fresh dill
1/2 teaspoon minced fresh oregano (or 1/4 teaspoon dried)
1/4 teaspoon freshly ground black pepper
1/4 teaspoon minced fresh basil
GRILLED GARLIC BBQ CHICKEN
1 1/3 tablespoons olive oil
1 1/3 tablespoons minced garlic
2 teaspoons soy sauce
2 teaspoons salt

4 5-ounce boneless, skinless chicken breasts
1/4 cup good-quality bottled sweet-and-spicy barbecue sauce
SALAD
1/2 head iceberg lettuce, cored, rinsed, dried, and cut into 1/8-inch-wide strips
1/2 head Romaine lettuce leaves, separated and trimmed, rinsed, dried, and cut into 1/8-inch-wide strips
12 large fresh basil leaves, cut into 1/8-inch-wide strips
1 pound jicama, cut into 1/4-inch cubes
2 cups shredded Monterey Jack cheese
1 cup canned black beans, rinsed and drained
1 cup canned sweet white corn kernels, drained
3 tablespoons chopped fresh cilantro
2 pounds ripe fresh tomatoes, cut into 1/8-inch dice
1/2 cup good-quality bottled sweet-and-spicy barbecue sauce
1/4 cup thinly sliced scallion greens

For fried tortilla strips:
• In a deep, heavy frying pan, heat several inches of vegetable oil to a temperature of 375 degrees. Working in batches if necessary to prevent overcrowding, carefully add tortilla strips to hot oil, submerging them with a metal skimmer or slotted spoon. Fry tortilla strips until evenly golden, 1 to 2 minutes. Carefully lift them out with skimmer or slotted spoon and transfer them to paper towels to drain and cool. Set aside, uncovered.

For garden herb ranch dressing:
• In a mixing bowl, use a fork to stir together the mustard and cold water, forming a paste. Set aside for 10 minutes. Add all remaining dressing ingredients to bowl and, using a handheld electric mixer at low speed or a whisk, blend together just until smooth, taking care not to incorporate too much air into dressing. Cover with plastic wrap and refrigerate.

For grilled garlic BBQ chicken:
Preheat a stovetop grill or broiler. In a mixing bowl, stir together olive oil, garlic, soy sauce, and salt. Turn chicken breasts in marinade and leave to marinate at room temperature for about 15 minutes. Grill or broil chicken breasts until cooked through, 5 to 6 minutes per side. Chill thoroughly in refrigerator. Cut chicken breasts into 3/4-inch cubes and, in a bowl, toss with barbecue sauce to coat well. Cover with plastic wrap and refrigerate.

For salad:
In a large mixing bowl, toss together lettuces, basil, jicama, Monterey Jack cheese, beans, corn, cilantro, Garden Herb Ranch Dressing, and half the Fried Tortilla Strips. Transfer salad to chilled serving plates. Surround each salad with diced tomatoes and the remaining Fried Tortilla Strips. Top each salad with chunks of Grilled Garlic BBQ Chicken and drizzle the chicken with barbecue sauce. Garnish with scallions.

Makes 4 main courses or 8 appetizer servings

Recipe courtesy of California Pizza Kitchen, Inc.

El Tiempo Cantina's Chile Con Queso Estilo Mexicano

3 cups water (half-and-half or chicken stock can also be used)
7 1/2 pounds Velveeta
3 whole bell peppers, diced
2 stalks celery, diced
3 cups jarred pico de gallo

Heat Velveeta with liquid in a double boiler. When Velveeta is melted, add other ingredients. Serve with chips, nachos, or as a perfect dressing for your favorite dish.

Serves 15–20 people or more

Recipe courtesy of El Tiempo Cantina, Houston, Texas

Mr. Chow's Gold Leaf Dumplings

6 tablespoons wheat flour
4 tablespoons hot water
1 tablespoon custard powder
1 teaspoon lard (white)
2 tablespoons corn starch
100 grams fresh prawns (small), chopped to 4–6 pieces each
100 grams fresh chicken breast, ground and minced
1 tablespoon diced carrots
2 stems chives, chopped very fine

1/2 teaspoon salt
1/4 teaspoon ginger, chopped very fine
1/4 teaspoon white pepper
1/2 teaspoon powdered chicken stock
5 grams shark fin
8–12 pieces edible gold leaf (24 kt); gold pieces should be pinch size

For dough:
In a bowl, mix wheat flour with hot water slowly to make sure mixture is smooth. Add custard powder, lard, corn starch, mixed evenly. Place dough in a plastic bag to keep moisture in and put aside.

For filling:
In a bowl, combine shrimp, ground chicken breast, carrots, chives, salt, ginger, white pepper, and powdered chicken stock until all ingredients are mixed evenly.

For dumplings:
Make the prepared dough into a 6-to-7-inch diameter pancake. Add 1 1/2 teaspoons of filling in middle of each pancake and make a shape. Steam dumplings for approximately 7 minutes and place a few pieces of shark fin and a small piece (a pinch) of gold leaf on top of each to finish.

Serves 6

Recipe courtesy of Mr. Chow

SHAKEN AND STIRRED

Nobu Black Cod with Miso

4 black cod fillets, about 1/2 pound each
3 cups Nobu-style saikyo miso (recipe follows)
1 stalk hajikami per serving
NOBU-STYLE SAIKYO MISO
3/4 cup sake
3/4 cup mirin
2 cups white miso paste
1 1/4 cups sugar

For Nobu-style saikyo miso:
• In a medium sacepan over high heat, bring sake and mirin to a boil. Boil for about 20 seconds to evaporate the alcohol. Reduce heat to low and add miso paste, mixing with a wooden spoon.
• When miso has dissolved completely, raise heat to high again and add sugar, stirring constantly with wooden spoon to bottom of pan so sauce does not burn.
• Remove sauce from heat once sugar is completely dissolved and cool to room temperature.

For fish:
• Pat cod fillets thoroughly dry with a paper towel.
• Slather the fish with the Nobu-style saikyo miso and place in a nonreactive dish or bowl. Cover tightly with plastic wrap. Leave to steep in refrigerator 2 to 3 days.
• Preheat the oven to 400 degrees. Preheat grill or broiler. Lightly wipe off any excess miso clinging to fillets but do not rinse off. Place fish on grill or in a broiler pan, and grill or broil until surface of fish turns brown.
• Transfer fillets to an ovenproof pan or baking dish and bake for 10 to 15 minutes, until opaque.
• After fish is cooked, arrange black cod fillets on individual plates and garnish with hajikami. Add a few extra drops of Nobu-style saikyo miso to each plate.

Serves 4

Recipe courtesy of Nobu Restaurant

Mommy's Italian Cheese Loaf

2 garlic cloves
1 block cream cheese
1/2 stick butter
1 pound sliced provolone cheese (divided)
Pesto (basil, olive oil, garlic,

Pignoli), homemade or jarred
Sun-dried tomatoes, chopped
Fresh basil (for garnish)
Large plain crackers (Gilda recommended)

• In a food processor, chop garlic. Add cream cheese and butter. Set aside mixture.
• Line a loaf pan with a wet, light towel. Layer with slices of provolone cheese so that you have overlapping halves. Do this on sides as well. Spread half the pesto over cheese on bottom. Add another layer of provolone cheese, then sprinkle half the sun-dried tomatoes. Spread all garlic cream cheese mixture over tomatoes. Sprinkle other half of tomatoes. Place another layer of provolone cheese and fold over ends of cheese all around. Lightly press down.
• Cover the pan with Saran wrap, then foil. Refrigerate overnight.
• Remove foil and Saran wrap. Turn cheese loaf over on a gorgeous plate. Garnish with fresh basil. Place crackers all around the plate. Use a beautiful cheese knife.

Serves 15

Recipe courtesy of Lara's mother Felice

Mini Paris Cupcakes

CUPCAKES

3/4 cup self-rising flour
2/3 cup all-purpose flour
1/2 cup unsalted butter, softened
1 cup sugar
2 eggs
1/2 cup milk
1/2 teaspoon vanilla

FROSTING

1/2 cup unsalted butter, softened
1/4 cup milk
1 teaspoon vanilla extract
1 drop red food coloring
3–4 cups confectioners' sugar

For cupcakes:

Line 12 mini muffin tins with mini muffin papers. In a small bowl, combine flours. In another bowl, cream butter and sugar together, beating until fluffy. Add eggs and beat well. Add half flour mixture and beat well, then add milk and vanilla and beat again. Add remaining flour mixture and beat until completely incorporated. Fill muffin papers about 3/4 full. Preheat oven to 350 degrees. Bake for 10 to 15 minutes. Remove cupcakes from oven and let cool.

For frosting:

• Place butter, milk, vanilla, food coloring, and 2 cups of the confectioners' sugar in a mixing bowl. Beat on medium speed until smooth and creamy. Gradually add remaining sugar until light and fluffy.
• Ice tops of cupcakes with pink frosting. Serve on a beautiful tray or tiered cake plate.

Makes 12 cupcakes

Recipe courtesy of Kathleen Sacchi, The Fine Art of Catering

Mac 'n' Cheese Croquettes

2 cups premade macaroni and cheese
1 cup flour
Salt and pepper
2 eggs, beaten
1 cup panko bread crumbs
1/4 cup mayonnaise
1 clove garlic
2 teaspoons lemon juice
Canola oil for deep-frying

• Roll macaroni and cheese into bite-sized balls. Dredge balls in flour seasoned with salt and pepper. Tap off excess flour and dip in eggs, then panko. Let balls sit for a few minutes to set crust.
• In a separate bowl, mix together mayo, garlic, and lemon juice to make aioli.
• Heat oil in pan until it reaches 375 degrees. Very carefully drop balls into hot oil and fry until golden brown. Drain on paper towels.
• Serve croquettes on platter with small bowl of aioli dipping sauce.

Makes 2 dozen croquettes

Recipe courtesy of Kathleen Sacchi, The Fine Art of Catering

resource guide

Organically Good

INVITATIONS

Bernard Maisner
Envelopes, calligraphy, table cards, and menu cards
www.bernardmaisner.com

FOOD AND DRINKS

Chef Akasha Richmond
www.chefakasha.com

Earthbound Farms
Organic salads and fruits
800-690-3200
www.ebfarm.com

Silk soy milk
www.silkissoy.com

Elixir Tonics & Teas
www.elixirtonics.net

SERVING

Calvin Klein
Black dinner plates
www.calvinklein.com

Hermès
Glasses and flatware
www.hermes.com

Ikea
Demitasse cups
www.ikea.com

Missoni
Bowls
www.neimanmarcus.com

Takashimaya
Linen napkins
212-350-0100

Ralph Lauren
www.rlhome.polo.com

Z Gallerie
Black martini glasses
www.zgallerie.com

DÉCOR

Flowers
Eric Buterbaugh Flower Designs
www.ericbuterbaugh.com

LIGHTING

Creative Candles
Tall pillar candles
800-237-9711
www.creativecandles.com

Diptyque Candles
www.diptyqueusa.com

Ikea
Candlesticks, white tea lights, and red glass candleholders
www.ikea.com

Gift Bag
Avalon Organics
www.avalonnaturalproducts.com

Elixir Tonics & Teas gift set
www.elixirtonics.com

Oh, Sugar!

INVITATION

Robin Maguire
www.robinmaguire.com

FOOD AND DRINKS

Catering
Barts Carts
Cotton-candy cart, snow-cone cart, ice-cream cart, Frozen margarita machine
www.bartscarts.com

Sweets and Candy
The Fountain coffee shop
Chocolate-coconut cake
www.thebeverlyhillshotel.com

The Ivy
Carrot cake
310-274-8303

Joan's on Third
Cupcakes
323-655-2285
www.joansonthird.com

Krispy Kreme doughnuts
800-4KRISPY (800-457-4779)
www.krispykreme.com

Mrs. Beasley's
Miss Grace lemon cakes, assorted brownies and cookies
www.mrsbeasleys.com

Cookies by Design
888-882-6654
www.cookiesbydesign.com

Cold Stone Creamery
www.coldstonecreamery.com

Dylan's Candy Bar
www.dylanscandybar.com

Economy Candy
Old-school candy
800-352-4544
www.economycandy.com

Peterbrooke Chocolatier
Chocolate-covered pretzels
www.peterbrooke.com

Cocktails
Corzo tequila
www.corzo.com

SERVING

Ikea
Party décor, tables, and serving trays
www.ikea.com

Crate & Barrel
Acrylic glasses
www.crateandbarrel.com

PHOTOGRAPHY

Photo-Me
Photobooth
866-PHOTO-ME
(800-746-8663)
www.photo-me.com

Sitars and Samosas

INVITATIONS

Creative Intelligence, Inc.
www.creative-intelligence.com

FOOD AND DRINKS

Catering
The Fine Art of Catering
818-246-0300

Bombay Café
www.bombaycafe-la.com

Gavinda's
Ginger and White Rabbit candies
310-856-2676

Cocktails
Grey Goose vodka
www.greygoose.com

SERVING

Accoutrements
Who's Got the Monkey?
Cocktail-glass ornaments
www.accoutrements.com

DÉCOR

Raj Tents
www.rajtents.com

Jaipur Imports
www.indianfurnishings.com

World Market
Décor pillows, lanterns
www.worldmarket.com

Flowers
Eric Buterbaugh Flower Designs
www.ericbuterbaugh.com

Lighting
Lighten Up Inc.
310-670-8515
www.lightenupinc.com

Entertainment
Taal Dance Company
www.taaldance.com

Alien Chatter
Sitar, tabla, djembe, and manjari players
www.alienchatter.com

Gift bags
Delman
www.delmanshoes.com

Afternoon Splash

INVITATIONS

Paper Source
www.paper-source.com

FOOD AND DRINKS

The Fine Art of Catering
818-246-0300

Jelly Belly
Pink and green jelly beans
www.jellybelly.com

Jolly Ranchers
www.hersheys.com/jollyrancher

Cocktails
Grey Goose vodka
www.greygoose.com

DÉCOR

Flowers
Eric Buterbaugh Flower Designs
www.ericbuterbaugh.com

Inspiration
The Beverly Hills Hotel
www.thebeverlyhillshotel.com

For the Tweety Birds

INVITATIONS

Creative Intelligence
www.creative-intelligence.com

Paper Source
Envelopes and yellow paper
www.paper-source.com

Party on La Cienega
310-659-8717

Kate's Paperie
www.katespaperie.com

LOCATION

Kitson
www.shopkitson.com

Scoop
www.scoopnyc.com

FOOD AND DRINKS

The Fine Art of Catering
818-246-0300

Dessert and candy
Cookies by Design
888-882-6654
www.cookiesbydesign.com

Twinkies
www.twinkies.com

Yellow candy
www.candyfavorites.com
www.economycandy.com

Yellow M&Ms
www.mms.com

Lemonheads
www.ferrarapan.com

Cocktails
Grey Goose vodka
www.greygoose.com

Planet Sugar
Lemon Twist Cocktail Candy
323-276-3905
www.cocktailcandy.com

Snapple lemonade
800-SNAPPLE (800-762-7753)
www.snapple.com

Voss water
www.vosswater.com

SERVING

Amscam
Yellow cups and plates
800-444-8887 (order line)
www.amscam.com

Crate and Barrel
Acrylic serving trays
www.crateandbarrel.com

Accoutrements
Black Cat swizzle sticks
425-349-3838
www.accoutrements.com

DÉCOR

Tweety products
Warner Brothers
www.warnerbros.com

Junk Food Tweety T-shirts
www.shopkitson.com
www.scoopnyc.com

Amscam
Yellow balloons, candles
800-444-8887
www.amscam.com

Paper Mart
Yellow cellophane and plastic
800-745-8800
www.papermart.com

Yellow feathers
www.featherplace.com
www.michaels.com

Petco
Birdcages
www.petco.com

Paper Source
Pressed-petal confetti
www.papersource.com

Yellow balloons
www.1-800-balloons.com
www.balloons.com

Mrs. Grossman's stickers
www.esticker.com
www.mrsgrossmans.com

Flowers
Eric Buterbaugh Flower Design
www.ericbuterbaugh.com

Music
DJ Samantha Ronson
www.samantharonson.com

Party Princess

INVITATIONS

Robin Maguire
800-922-2259
www.robinmaguire.com

Party on La Cienega
310-659-8717

Paper Source
888-PAPER-11
www.paper-source.com

Envelopes
www.paperandmore.com
www.paper-source.com

Sand Scripts
Envelope seals
www.sandscripts.com

Mrs. Grossman's stickers
www.esticker.com
www.mrsgrossmans.com

Happy-birthday stamps
www.usps.com

Birthday-party supplies
Kid Stuff.com
Fun food packaging,
marketing ideas
www.kidstuff.com

Birthday Express
Ultimate kids' birthday-party
suppliers
www.1800birthday.com

LOCATION

Crobar
www.crobar.com

Car service
www.newyorkluxurylimo.com

Manicures
BuffSpa
www.buffspa.com

Hair
John Barrett Salon
www.johnbarrett.com

Makeup
Shu Uemura
888-SHU-5678 (888-748-5678)
www.shuuemura-usa.com

FOOD AND DRINKS

Pop Burger
212-414-8686

Two Boots Pizza
www.twoboots.com
212-254-1919

Domino's Pizza
www.dominos.com

Pizza Hut
www.pizzahut.com

Appetizers to Go
Pigs in a blanket
800-757-0058
www.appetizerstogo.com

Dessert
Buttercup Bake Shop
Red velvet cupcakes with cream-
cheese frosting
www.buttercupbakeshop.com

Krispy Kreme doughnuts
800-4KRISPY (800-457-4779)
www.krispykreme.com

Cookies by Design
888-882-6654
www.cookiesbydesign.com

Candy
Wonka Laffy Taffy
www.candydirect.com

Jolly Ranchers
www.hersheys.com/jollyrancher

Foreign Candy Company
Green-apple Rip Rolls
www.foreign-candy.com

Dryden & Palmer
Rock-Candy Crystal Sticks in lime
www.rockcandy.com
www.candyDirect2U.com

SERVING

Silver serving tray
www.williams-sonoma.com
www.target.com
www.silverheaven.com
www.unicahome.com

Hermès
Small green glass tumblers
www.hermes.com

Capri Sun Tropical punch cooler
www.kraftfoods.com/caprisun

DÉCOR

Amscan
Balloons
800-446-8887
www.amscan.com

Balloon Delivery USA
www.balloondeliveryusa.com

Bobble-head dolls
866-775-3985
www.bobbleheadworld.com

Sparkler candles
800-444-8887
www.amscan.com

ENTERTAINMENT

Party Poopers
Party Poopers is a full-service party-
planning organization covering all
types of parties, from kids' birthdays,
to intimate adult dinners, to funky
anniversaries, to corporate family pic-
nics and special events.
Break-dance instruction, games
877-PARTY POOPERS
www.partypoopers.com

Music
DJ Shrifty
Contact: Jonathan Shriftman
djshrifty@aol.com

Games
Nintendo games
www.nintendo.com

Photography
Hewlett-Packard digital
cameras
www.hp.com

Let the Fur Fly!

FOOD AND DRINKS

Taverna Tony Greek Eats
and Sweets
310-317-9667

Desserts
Romolo Chocolates
Romolo Chocolates provided gourmet "puppy chow" and chocolate
dog bones served in cookie jars, for
human guests.
www.romolochocolates.com

Dreyer's Dibs
www.dreyers.com

Cold Stone Creamery
www.coldstonecreamery.com

Sour Punch Candy
Blue Raspberry Sour Punch Straws were used as stirrers in the drinks.
www.sourpunch.com

Three Dog Bakery
800-4TREATS
www.threedog.com

SERVING

Crate and Barrel
White serving dishes, small turquoise bowls, plates, shot glasses and cups, cookie jars, glass plates, and white tubs
www.crateandbarrel.com

Fred Segal
Large black-and-white glass Fred Segal serving dishes.
323-651-4129

Takashimaya
Takashimaya bowls were used for the hummus dip from Taverna Tony.
www.takashimaya.com

Fifi & Romeo
Fifi and Romeo provided doggy table coverings with miniature-poodle stuffed animals as centerpieces.
323-857-7215
www.fifandromeo.com

Tiffany & Co.
Silver platters
www.tiffany.com

DÉCOR

Flowers
Eric Buterbaugh Flower Design
www.ericbuterbaugh.com

Alba Organics sun-care products
www.albabotanica.com

H₂O Plus Face Oasis mist
www.h2oplus.com

Music
DJ Jonathan Shriftman
djshrifty@aol.com

ACTIVITIES

Kelly's Pet Care
This dog-walking company entertained the dogs while the guests ate.
800-618-5584
www.kpc.us

TLC Mobile Pet Grooming Service
This pet-grooming company

---

provided a station for guest's dogs to get shampooed and groomed.
323-730-0378

OPI
OPI provided a "peticure" station onsite for all the dogs.
800-341-9999
www.opi.com

Hewlett-Packard photo station
Hewlett-Packard provided a photo station so guests could take pictures with their dogs.
800-752-0900
www.hp.com

Gift Bags
Victoria's Secret Pink
Victoria's Secret provided pj's and sweatsuit outfits named after each dog and pink polka-dot dog outfits wrapped in pink tissue paper.
www.victoriassecret.com

Fifi & Romeo
The froufou doggy boutique offers decadent goods made for pint-sized pooches. This boutique carries items such as blankets, raincoats, and stylish doggy totes. At our party the pet boutique gave an assortment of gifts for pets and humans.
323-857-7215

Poker Party

LOCATION

W. Los Angeles Westwood
310-208-8765
www.whotels.com

INVITATIONS

Cartier
Invitation
www.cartier.com

The Poker Room
Clay poker chips
www.thepokerroomnewyork.com

Menu Cards
Robin Maguire
Drink Menu Cards
www.robinmaguire.com

FOOD & DRINKS

Catering
Nine Thirty (W Hotel)
www.whotels.com

The Cake Divas
Cupcakes
310-287-2609
www.cakedivas.com

Cookies by Design
Poker chip cookies
888-882-6654
www.cookiesbydesign.com

Dylan's Candy Bar
Candy
www.dylanscandybar.com

Cocktails
Whiskey Blue
www.whotels.com

Grey Goose Vodka
www.greygoosevodka.com

Corzo Tequila
www.corzo.com

Macallan
Scotch
www.themacallan.com

Godiva Liquer
Chocolate Liquer
www.godiva.com/liquer/main.asp

Moët and Chandon
Mini bottles of champagne
www.moet.com

Elixir Tonics & Teas
Tonics
877.4ELIXIR
www.elixirtonics.com

DÉCOR

The Poker Room
This luxury poker shop provided hand-made Italian poker tables valued at $18k each, clay poker chips, and playing cards.
212-625-1170
www.thepokerroomnewyork.com

Flowers and Candles
Eric Buterbaugh Flower Design
Flowers
www.ericbuterbaugh.com

Ikea
Floating Candles
800-434-IKEA
www.ikea.com

SERVICES

Bliss spa
Hand massages and spa products
www.blissworld.com

Kenn Woodard
Astrological readings
310-409-7148

WooGuy Cigar and Smoke Shop
323-650-2920
www.wooguycigarshop.com

The Poker Room
Poker lessons, playing cards, and clay poker chips
212-625-1170
www.thepokerroomnewyork.com

Playboy Playing Cards
www.playboyplayingcards.com

Winner's Prize
2-night stay at the W Hotel
www.whotels.com

Grey Goose martini set
www.greygoosevodka.com

Corzo Tequila VIP kit
www.corzo.com

Nintendo DS system with "World Championship Poker Deluxe Series"
www.nintendo.com

Gift Bags
Signed copy of *Annie Duke: How I Raised, Folded, Bluffed, Flirted, Cursed and Won Millions at the World Series of Poker*
www.amazon.com

Bliss
www.blissworld.com

WooGuy Cigar & Smoke Shop
323-650-2920
www.wooguycigarshop.com

The Poker Room
212-625-1170
www.thepokerroomnewyork.com

Robin Maguire Poker Notepads
Stationery
www.robinmaguire.com

UltimateBet.com
Poker mousepad and hat
www.ultimatebet.com

Shaken and Stirred

LOCATION

The Beverly Hills Hotel Polo Lounge
310-276-2251
www.thebeverlyhillshotel.com

INVITATION

Creative Intelligence
Contact: Marc Friedland
www.creative-intelligence.com

CATERING

The Beverly Hills Hotel
www.thebeverlyhillshotel.com

Nobu
www.nobumatsuhisa.com

Cocktails
Grey Goose vodka
www.greygoose.com

Flowers
Eric Buterbaugh Flower Designs
310-247-7120
www.ericbuterbaugh.com

DJ
Samantha Ronson
www.samantharonson.com

Gift bag
UGG Australia
888-432-8530
www.uggaustralia.com

Yahoo! Personals
Dating-service website
T-shirts for gift bags
personals.yahoo.com

Le Tigre T-shirts
www.holdthattiger.com

Dr. Raj Kanodia
Plastic surgery
310-409-7148
www.drkanodia.com

Aura reading
Contact: Kenn Woodward
skywritfire@aol.com

PHOTOGRAPHY

Photo station
Polaroid photography
Contact: Arthur Africano
323-605-3939

Best Host Gifts

BOOKS

First-edition books
www.alibris.com
www.baumanrarebooks.com

Entertaining books
Ina Garten books
www.barefootcontessa.com

Fête Accompli! The Ultimate Guide to Creative Entertaining
www.feteaccompli.net

Jackie Collins novels
www.amazon.com
www.barnesandnoble.com

Photo albums and scrapbooks
Ronnie Gousman
323-651-2900

Restaurant cookbooks
www.joesstonecrab.com
www.ecookbooks.com

GIFT CERTIFICATES
Calligraphy
Stephannie Barba
Couture calligraphy &
stationery
415-437-6001
www.stephanniebarba.com

Bernard Maisner
www.bernardmaisner.com

Beauty salons
Frederic Fekkai Salon
www.fredericfekkai.com

Oribe Salon
www.oribesalon.com

John Barrett Salon
www.johnbarrett.com

Day spas
Bliss Spas
www.blissworld.com/spa

BuffSpa
www.buffspa.com

The Four Seasons Day Spas
www.fourseasons.com

Cornelia Day Spa
www.cornelia.com

Private training
Equinox fitness clubs
www.equinoxfitness.com

Burn 60
burn60.com

S Factor
www.sfactor.com

Music
www.apple.com/itunes
www.towerrecords.com
www.virginrecords.com

Books
www.amazon.com
www.barnesandnoble.com

Catering and private chefs
Akasha Richmond
www.chefakasha.com

Movies
www.amazon.com
www.barnesandnoble.com
www.netflix.com

FOOD & DRINKS
Arrowhead Mountain Spring
Water
www.arrowheadwater.com

Poland Spring
www.polandspring.com

Sparkletts
www.sparkletts.com

Serendipity 3 frrrozen hot chocolate
800-805-5493
www.williams-sonoma.com
www.serendipity3.com

Mrs. Beasley's
Miss Grace lemon cakes
www.mrsbeasleys.com

Eli's Essentials
www.elizabar.com

Starbucks
www.starbucks.com

The Coffee Bean & Tea Leaf
gift set
800-TEA-LEAF (800-832-5323)
www.coffeebean.com

A Basket of sauces
Nobu
www.nobumatsuhisa.com

Raos
www.raos.com

Giorgio Baldi
www.giorgiobaldi.com

Peter Luger
www.peterluger.com

Jean-Georges Vongerichten
www.jean-georges.com

PERSONALIZED STATIONERY AND THANK-YOU CARDS
Tiffany & Co.
www.tiffany.com

Cartier
www.cartier.com

Mrs. John L. Strong
www.barneys.com

Smythson of Bond Street
www.smythson.com

The Wren Press
www.wrenpress.com

PICTURE FRAMES
Ralph Lauren
www.rlhome.polo.com

Calvin Klein Home
800-294-7978

PHOTOGRAPHY
Hewlett-Packard
Photo camera and printer
www.hp.com

Customized iPod
Apple
www.apple.com/ipod

Best Buy
www.bestbuy.com

Circuit City
www.circuitcity.com

TOBACCO
Nat Sherman colored cigarettes
www.natsherman.com

ROBES AND SLIPPERS
Kashwére
www.kashwere.com

CANDLES
Calvin Klein Home
800-294-7978

Votivo Candles
www.sensia.com
www.shopkitson.com

Slatkin & Co. Candles
www.scentedboutique.com

Diptyque Candles
www.beautyhabit.com

Creative Candles
www.creativecandles.com

Ted Muehling candlesticks
212-431-3825

INCENSE
XELA Aromasticks
800-554-0826
www.xelaaromasticks.com

C. Z. Guest
www.slatkin.com

D.L. & Co.
818-989-0035
www.dlcompany.com

DINNERWARE
Calvin Klein Home
800-294-7978

Hermès
www.hermes.com

Ralph Lauren
www.rlhome.polo.com

GLASSWARE
Baccarat
www.neimanmarcus.com

Saint-Louis
www.michaelcfina.com

LOTTERY TICKETS
Interlotto
www.interlotto.com

GAMES
Twister
www.areyougame.com

Monopoly
www.hasbro.com/monopoly

FAO Schwarz
www.fao.com

MAGAZINE SUBSCRIPTIONS
www.magazines.com
www.magsdirect.com

acknowledgments

Special thanks to Betty Wong and Jill Cohen at Bulfinch Press; Doug Turshen, our art director, for being so helpful and supportive throughout this entire project; and David Huang. Thanks to all the Harrison & Shriftman staff in New York, LA, and Miami, especially Michelle McConnell for being so amazing, detail oriented, and perfect. Thanks to Kristen Blucas, Hilary Broderick, and Kristy Tatem, for producing all of our great parties; Rachel Shapiro, Erika Koopman, Andrea Kasparoff, Vanessa Poskanzer, Jose Martinez, Halle Reum, Ilia Saddler, Liz Keen, Don Luciano, Angie Banicki, Jamie Henderson, Lauren Gould, and Jennifer Mazur.

Thanks to all the photographers at WireImage, including Jeff Vespa, Donato Sardella, Stephen Lovekin, Chris Pizzello, John Shearer, Jamie McCarthy, Dimitrios Kambouris, Deverill Weekes, and Amy Graves.

Special thanks to Jeff Vespa, John Shearer, Andrea Collins and Matthew Roberts for all of their time and support.

Thanks to everyone who gave us tips, including Alana Stewart, Billy Bob Thornton, Dani Janssen, David Arquette, Jackie Collins, Jennifer Finnigan, Lara Flynn Boyle, Forest and Keisha Whitaker, Annie Duke, Kristin Cavallari, Maeve Quinlan, Michael Michele, Michael Kors, Molly Sims, Nicky Hilton, Peter Som, Sarah Michelle Gellar, Stephen Dorff, Luke Wilson, and Regina King.

Thanks to everyone who gave us fabulous recipes: Kathleen Sacchi of The Fine Art of Catering; Chef Akasha Richmond, Nicki B. Reiss, and Sergio Gomez; Taverna Tony; Cary Richardson; Erica Matsunaga from Nobu in Malibu; Nobu Matsuhisa; Sasha Tcherevkoff; Shareef Malnik and Maxwell Blandford from the Forge; Privé; Elixir Tonics & Teas; Anastasia Williams; Eva and Michael Chow from Mr. Chow; David Copperfield; Noah Tepperberg from Marquee; Nine Thirty; and Rande Gerber from Whiskey Blue.

Thanks to Eric Buterbaugh, for the beautiful flowers and tips; Anna Bisson; Alejandro Rivera and Amy Cotteleer, for fabulous décor at the Paris Hilton fragrance launch in LA and at the Juicy Couture; Bernard Maisner, for his classic invitations and calligraphy; Robin McGuire, for all of her great invitations; Mark Friedland; Jonathan Shriftman; Rob Sheiffele, Lisa Gregorich-Dempsey, and Debbie Haderle at *Extra*. Kelli Delaney for her constant support; Melissa Weiner; Michael Rosenberg; Allison Sarofim, for being such a great hostess; Yana Syrkin and Owen Swady from Fifi & Romeo; Ryan Drexler; Susan Campos; Dr. Raj Kanodia; Kristin Scott; Doug Geller; and Eliane Henri.

Thanks to everyone who let us shoot their parties: Karine Joret and Barry Ziehl; Stephanie Greenfield at Scoop; Frazier Ross at Kitson; Serena Williams; Rita, Ava, Sophia, and Ian Schrager; Ron and Cheryl Howard; Brian and Gigi Grazer; Pam Skaist-Levy and Gela Taylor; Rosemary De Loranzo Swimwear Anywear Inc.; Scott Rudin; Allison Jackson; Paris Hilton; Ilia Lekach at Parlux Fragrances; Ross Klein, Jane Lehman, Melissa Brown, and Jenni Benzaquen at the W Hotel.

Special thanks to all of our amazing parents for always entertaining us.

PHOTO CREDITS

Organically Good: A Dinner Party at Home
Jeff Vespa / WireImage
Oh, Sugar! A Delicious Party
Jeff Vespa / WireImage
John Shearer / WireImage
Sitars and Samosas: The Perfect Indian Fête
Jeff Vespa / WireImage
Donato Sardella / WireImage
Amy Graves / WireImage
Afternoon Splash: Sun and Fun, Poolside
Jeff Vespa / WireImage
Donato Sardella / WireImage

For the Tweety Birds: A Mellow Yellow Shopping Soiree
Donato Sardella / WireImage
John Shearer / WireImage
Party Princess: A Kid's Birthday
Stephen Lovekin / WireImage
Let the Fur Fly! A Party for a Dog's Best Friend
Amy Graves / WireImage
Poker Party: Boys' Night Out
John Shearer / WireImage
Shaken and Stirred: A Classic Cocktail Party (LA)
Donato Sardella / WireImage
Jamie McCarthy / WireImage

It's a Pleasure Doing Business: A Product Launch Party (LA)
Jeff Vespa / WireImage
Jamie McCarthy / WireImage
It's a Pleasure Doing Business: A Product Launch Party (NY)
Dimitrios Kambouris / WireImage

Additional Credits
Andrea Collins, Photo Producer
Deverill Weekes, Photo Assistant

Additional Photographers
Chris Pizzello / WireImage
Bob Levey / WireImage
Paul Costello, page 7

ABOUT THE AUTHORS

Lara Shriftman and **Elizabeth Harrison** are the principals at the high-profile public-relations, special-events, and marketing firm Harrison & Shriftman, with offices in New York, Los Angeles, and Miami. Famous for branding companies, marketing, and generating A-list publicity, their special-events division has produced many highly publicized events, including movie premieres for *Charlie's Angels, Bridget Jones's Diary,* and *Legally Blonde;* store openings for Michael Kors, Scoop, and Hogan; charity events for Love Heals, American Ballet Theatre, and Toys for Tots; fashion shows for Oscar de la Renta, Jill Stuart, and Lacoste; and product launches for Cartier, Calvin Klein, Juicy Couture, and L.A.M.B. After the release of their books *Fête Accompli! The Ultimate Guide to Creative Entertaining* and *Fête Accompli! Workbook: The Ultimate Party Planning Guide,* Lara and Elizabeth were touted as experts in magazines including *Vanity Fair, Glamour, Seventeen,* and *Departures,* on television shows such as *Extra,* and on channels including Fox, CNN, and E! Entertainment Television.

Lara Morgenson is an editor and a columnist for E! Online and lives in Los Angeles. Each week she dishes about her party-hopping lifestyle and A-list happenings in her column "Hollywood Party Girl." It's the perfect outlet for chronicling her passions for fashion, celebrities, and parties. She covers each soiree in glamorous detail, from the decadent décor and stylish guests to the gourmet delicacies and martini of the moment. She's stepped behind the velvet rope at countless celebrity-driven events, including the Golden Globes, the Emmys, and the Academy Awards, as well as at film premieres and at openings of exclusive clubs, restaurants, and boutiques. In addition, she frequently appears on E! Entertainment Television to share her celebrity and party expertise.

Bulfinch Press

Hachette Book Group USA
1271 Avenue of the Americas
New York, NY 10020
Visit our Web site at
www.bulfinchpress.com

First Edition: November 2006

    Library of Congress Cataloging-in-Publication Data
Shriftman, Lara.
  Party confidential / Lara Shriftman & Elizabeth Harrison with Lara Morgenson; photographed by Jeff Vespa. — 1st ed.
    p. cm.
  Includes index.
  ISBN-13: 978-0-8212-5780-7 (hardcover)
  ISBN-10: 0-8212-5780-3 (hardcover)
  1. Entertaining. 2. Parties—Planning. 3. Party decorations.
   I. Harrison, Elizabeth. II. Morgenson, Lara. III. Title.
  TX731 .S46 2006
  642'.4—dc22   2005032288

Design by Doug Turshen with David Huang

PRINTED IN SINGAPORE